BEYOND THE CLASSROOM:
INFORMING OTHERS

BEYOND THE CLASSROOM:
INFORMING OTHERS

A Music Educators National Conference Southern Division Special Project

Robert W. Surplus and James E. Dooley, Co-Chairmen
Committee Members: Robert R. Gaskins, Richard M. Graham, Charles R. Hoffer, and Jeanne Moore

Photographs on cover and title pages courtesy of:

Top left: Fairfax County Office of Public Affairs

Top right: National Association of Secondary School Principals

Bottom right: U.S. House of Representatives

Center: Linda Rutledge

Acknowledgements

The preparation of this publication involved numerous music educators from the Southern Division of the Music Educators National Conference. The project was planned and implemented by the MENC Southern Division Special Project Committee. This committee was co-chaired by Robert W. Surplus, Kentucky, and James E. Dooley, North Carolina, and also included Robert R. Gaskins, North Carolina, Richard M. Graham, Georgia, Charles R. Hoffer, Florida, and Jeanne Moore, West Virginia.

In addition to members of the Special Project Committee, thirteen music educators from throughout the Southern Division were invited to contribute to the project. Their ideas and written materials have been incorporated with those of the committee in the final version of the book. These individuals deserve recognition for their work, and their names are listed below.

Mildred Berkey.....................................Kentucky
Elinor Copenhaver............................West Virginia
Frank Crockett.......................................Georgia
Mary Jo Deaver....................................Alabama
Howard A. Doolin...................................Florida
James Draper...Georgia
William C. Fox...............................West Virginia
Billigene Garner............................North Carolina
Charles L. Gary.....................................Virginia
Dale K. Jensen.......................................Florida
Barbara Kaplan....................................Alabama
John W. Otwell......................................Georgia
Thomas L. Walters..................................Florida

Contents

foreword

This book has been prepared for use by music educators. It is one of a series of publications resulting from an emphasis on professional development begun by the Southern Division of MENC at its 1983 in-service conference held in Louisville, Kentucky.

The purpose of this publication is to provide practical help to music educators who are aware that success in their programs often depends not only on how well they teach music but also on how effectively they are able to work and interact with a wide range of individuals and groups. Some of the most important individuals and groups have been identified and described in this book, and guidance is offered for cultivating productive relationships with them. The information and suggestions included are drawn from the experience and accomplishments of successful music educators who were invited to prepare material for use in this project.

The MENC Southern Division Special Project Committee sends this publication forth in the hope that it will encourage and help music educators to extend their influence beyond the classroom, using their communicative and persuasive skills to inform others that music is a right of all children and young people. The impact of an individual music educator's role in this effort can be significant--that of a united profession is incalculable.

Introduction

Why This Book is for You

Check your profession:

( ) Band Director
( ) Choral Director
( ) General Music Teacher
( ) Orchestra Director
( ) Music Supervisor

No matter which item you checked or how many items you checked, you are a special kind of a teacher. You are a music educator–that is important.

A music educator, while specializing in one or more of the areas listed above, has an overall commitment to the music education of all students through a comprehensive program that includes general music, performance, and nonperformance elective areas of study. A music educator recognizes that no segment of the program stands alone. Each is important if young people with different needs, interests, and learning styles are to be given opportunities to develop skills, understandings, and attitudes in music.

This book has been written because serious concerns have arisen about the quality of music education in America. For too long music educators have failed to inform the public about the value and purpose of the school music program. Many music teachers assume either that it is someone else's job or that it doesn't need to be done. One result of this failure to inform is the present good news/bad news situation of music educaion. The good news is that some music instruction is found in almost all school districts, but the bad news is that the music curriculum is a far cry from what it should or could be. A few school districts have balanced, quality music programs, but many offer only a limited program. If music education in America is to improve, music educators must devote more attention to informing and winning over the public.

The problem is that many of America's children are not receiving adequate music instruction that is essential to a basic education--a right that belongs to all our youth. It is sad to say that this situation exists under the guidance of credentialed music specialists.

There are numerous reasons as to why this problem exists. For example, there are not enough music educators to meet the needs of America's children. In many school districts around the country, only a substantial increase in resources would provide the number of specialists needed to constitute a fully developed program and to extend the program to those students receiving little or no formal music instruction. Another part of the problem is the limited time available for music in the school day and the related difficulty of including music credits in graduation requirements.

While the total number of students in America who are involved in school music programs is substantial, students are deprived of the benefits of a comprehensive music curriculum. Significant numbers of students involved in music make their way through school with minimal exposure to professionally planned, guided learning experiences. It is paradoxical that in this, the wealthiest nation in the world, budgetary limitations are most often cited as the main reason for the lack of qualified personnel and quality music education programs.

To deal with this matter, music educators must enlist the assistance of all groups that can influence elected and appointed officials who determine budget priorities in the schools. The rationale for this effort is clear:

1. Without a comprehensive music education program, America's children are being deprived of learning experiences essential to their complete education.
2. Without adequate funding, a school cannot be expected to provide a comprehen - sive music program.

The problem of the lack of quality music programs can be dealt with directly by the individual music educator. One major difficulty that has emerged within the profession during the past several years is the separation between music teachers themselves. A division of effort has developed in the formation of single focus organizations within the profession. These groups focus on medium (choral, instrumental), methodology (Kodàly, Suzuki), type of music (jazz, classical), or instrument. The proliferation of separate band directors' organizations at the state level is one example of this fragmen - tation.

The result, or perhaps the cause, of these specialty organizations has been a lack of a comprehensive approach to music education programs. One can understand, and perhaps even sympathize with, the superintendent who is reluctant to increase the music education budget when approached not by a single representative but by several individuals who identify themselves as "Orff specialists," "jazz educators," "class piano teachers," "string or Suzuki teachers," "Kodàly experts," and so forth.

Special emphasis organizations are a valuable asset to the profession. They provide information about materials, techniques, philosophies, trends, and insights related to one's teaching concentration. They provide the strong reinforcement and encourage - ment that comes from close association with colleagues, especially those whose rich experience and outstanding abilities serve as powerful motivators for less experienced teachers.

Many individuals, however, are caught up in their enthusiasm for personal achieve -ment and high level accomplishment for their performing groups. They lose sight of their role in advancing the cause of music for all students. The ancient adage "you can't see the forest for the trees," certainly applies to many music teachers when their intense focus on one or two facets of the music curriculum obscures their vision of the total program and the need for developing and providing music learning experiences for all students.

As valuable as each special area may be, music educators can never hope for broad acceptance and support until all work toward the same goal. A united commitment to the concept of music for all students is essential. It must begin with each music educator. No one else is in a position to bring about the needed changes.

A second major difficulty that music educators must deal with is the lack of under -standing many school administrators, board members, teachers of other subjects, and members of the community have about music in the schools. This is one of the reasons why school systems often do not provide the administrative direction and resources necessary for a comprehensive music education program.

All music educators have encountered people who have only vague ideas why music is taught in the schools. Every music educator would like to teach in a system in which administrators, board members, and all members of the school staff know what music education is about. Every music educator would like to work in a community that supports music education. However, this is a less-than-perfect world, and there are many who do not know why music should be taught in the schools. They probably never have been informed.

The remedy for this deficiency is to reach these people and make them aware that music should be a part of the basic curriculum. Programs should be provided that con -firm the importance of music in the human experience and justify its inclusion as a subject for study by all students on the basis of its intrinsic value.

This book is written for you, the individual music educator. You and your col -leagues possess the interest, knowledge, understanding and dedication to meet the challenge. You are the professional who is most able to deliver the right message to the right people in the best ways. You, above all others, are able to generate the cohesive -ness within the profession essential to an integrated, focused effort. You know the administrators and teachers in your school. You live in the community, and people know you. They learn from you, and their children learn in your classes. Who else could speak so knowledgeably about music education? You are the resident expert and the person best qualified to inform those you know about music education.

Granted, you and your colleagues in music education are very busy. You have to plan lessons, give tests, grade papers, assign grades, keep attendance records, and maintain an effective classroom environment. Beyond that, you have unique responsibilities that range from repairing instruments to evaluating newly published music. Music educators are expected to be familiar with standardized music aptitude and achievement tests, where to obtain and how to administer them, and how to use the test results. Music educators also should know something about acoustics since they may be called upon to work with architects designing new music buildings or classrooms.

In addition to all other duties, many music educators must demonstrate the achievements of students in a number of public performances each year. Performances furnish evidence to school personnel, parents, and the public that music students are continually increasing their knowledge, understanding, and skills. Preparation for a performance usually involves the music educator in a number of nonmusical activities such as preparing the printed program, arranging for risers and the acoustical shell, and managing the tickets. It is not surprising that you may protest your overloaded schedule. But remember that you are more than just a choral director, a band director or a string specialist. You are a music educator and you must speak for the total program.

The information and suggestions provided here will give music educators the resources to speak with clarity and conviction about the purpose and value of music education and collectively develop the broad-based support that will be necessary for the development of comprehensive music programs.

The contribution of each music educator is important. While you may not be able to do everything outlined here, you can identify the tasks that lie within your abilities and pursue them with determination.

Points to remember

1. The children of America are too important to be denied the musical experiences available in a comprehensive music education program. Music study has been and continues to be recognized as a legitimate subject in a basic curriculum, and all students share the inherent right to receive quality instruction in music.

2. Music educators have an important role to play in the effort to effect change.

3. Music educators must work together to develop support and understanding for a music education program that meets the needs of all the students. Band directors, Suzuki specialists, choral directors, general music teachers, and all the others who concentrate in a specialized area of music study must join forces to promote all facets of a comprehensive program.

4. Music educators must assume responsibilities beyond the classroom. The mes - sage must be communicated to a wide variety of constituent groups that influ - ence the degree of acceptance for music study in the curriculum and the extent of support that your programs will receive in the future.

What is the Message?

Music educators often face this question: How do you explain the importance and purpose of music education to people who know little about music? Do you launch into an involved philosophical discourse filled with polysyllabic terms and vague concepts? Do you give reasons that have little to do with music and are not supported by research, evidence, or logic? Do you assume that music education is simply something that nonmusicians should accept on faith?

Let us begin by examining the aforementioned questions. Understanding the philo - sophical/psychological basis of the importance of music in human life is desirable, but the topic is enormously complex and does not lend itself to short, quick explanations. Unless the purpose is to bewilder the listener, the philosophical approach is ineffective, and often leaves the impression that you are attempting to cover up fuzzy thinking with a mountain of verbiage.

Claiming a variety of nonmusical benefits--citizenship, health, or academic ability-- is also not very effective. There are at least three reasons for this fact:

1. Only limited research evidence is available that supports the claim that gains in other areas of the school curriculum are a result of music study. Karen I. Wolff concludes, "While it is true that most of the research related to the nonmusical outcomes of music education has produced positive results, the conclusions drawn generally remain unconvincing. This is due largely to obvious inade - quacies in the experimental designs and also to the incomplete and equivocal descriptions of the experiments themselves." (*Council for Research of Music Education*, 1978)

2. Other areas of the curriculum or extracurricular activities are more successful in accomplishing the desired results. For example, courses in history and govern - ment are more pertinent to citizenship than are music courses, and physical education is more beneficial than music for health and fitness. If someone wishes to strengthen these areas, he or she is likely to select a means other than music instruction to do so.

3. Such claims detract from the most important reason for including music in the school curriculum--the aesthetic and psychological values. Science and English teachers do not justify their subjects by claiming that the students improve their health or general academic ability through the study of the subject, and neither should music educators. Science, English, and music all have value within the

school curriculum. Poorly supported claims for nonmusical outcomes only make music teachers appear weak, illogical, or uncertain about the values of their subject. If such claims turn out to be supportable, then the case for music will be that much stronger. However, a solid basis for including music in the schools can be built without making any claims for nonmusical benefits.

Certainly, music educators should not make the mistake of assuming that everyone supports school music just because they are told music is a good thing to have in the curriculum.

The main themes

What can music educators tell people about music education that meets the tests of being understandable and true? Both objective data and subjective intuition can be employed to do this.

First, let us examine the objective data. It is not difficult to support the fact that music and the other fine arts are important. Music is found as part the cultures of every people on the globe, from city dwellers to the remote desert aborigines of Australia. Furthermore, music has been pictured or described in every civilization. In present-day America millions of people play instruments and sing, and they spend vast sums of money for sound-reproducing equipment, records, and tapes. They also buy tickets to concerts; over 56 million adult Americans attend classical music concerts, opera, or musical plays (National Endowment for the Arts, 1984). Clearly, there must be some - thing important and valuable about an activity that is so widespread and sizable.

People in all places and times have demonstrated an important point--music is valuable to life. Music helps make life more interesting, satisfying, and meaningful; in short, it helps make people more human. If life were merely biological existence, then music would be an unnecessary frill. However, music and the other arts have much to do with the richness and quality of human life. It is in that sense that music is basic, vital, and valuable.

The intuitive, subjective case for music is evident in the fact that most people experience good feelings when they hear a group of children sing or play their instruments. They correctly sense that making music is a constructive, worthwhile thing for them to do. Most people are unable to say why they feel the way they do about music, but fortunately it is not necessary. This positive feeling is especially strong among parents who hear and observe their children perform music, as most music teachers can confirm. In fact, this feeling is so strong that parents are usually pleased when hearing their children even when the music is not rendered particularly well.

Objective evidence and intuitive feelings can be combined to promote positive feelings toward music instruction on the part of nonmusicians. The point to make is that young people should not be denied the opportunity to participate in and learn about music. This position might be called the "Let's not cheat the kids" approach. It is more than just an approach or technique, because students who have little or no music instruction in school are indeed being deprived of something valuable. Just as no one wants young people to grow up ignorant about science or unable to communicate clearly in writing or speech, no one should want them to go through life uninformed about music or unable to participate in it in a meaningful way. In a democracy all young people deserve the chance to learn about music. The only place where this chance can be assured is in the schools.

The "Let's not cheat the kids" approach has several commendable features. First, it focuses on the benefits to students. Music educators must be careful to avoid the appearance of promoting music because of the benefits to themselves in terms of jobs. Second, it is an approach that is easily understood; it doesn't require complex explana-tions or previous study in philosophy. Third, it is right. No young person should miss having the opportunity to learn about and be involved in music, because he or she would be missing something of value in life.

The need for quality instruction

The point about the value of music for all students is the first one to be established when informing people about the school music program. As important as that point is, a second point is also essential: music needs to be taught in a systematic and organized way by qualified teachers. As is true of science, English, and all other subject matter areas, if music is going to be experienced and studied beyond a rudimentary level, it needs to be taught by professionals. There is a great deal in music that is too complex for untrained people to teach. Without professional music instruction in the schools, the amount and type of music learned by most students would be a mere shadow of the subject as music educators know it.

The public's view of music education

When educating people about the purpose and value of music in the schools, it helps to keep in mind how they perceive school music. Some people see it primarily as publicly supported entertainment. They enjoy having groups that perform for various civic clubs and entertain at football or basketball games. These people need to understand that the entertainment activities of music organizations are fine, but they are not the main reason for the existence of music instruction in the schools.

Many people think of music only in terms of recreation or fun. Everyone needs some break from routine activities, and music is a good way to vary the routine. It needs to be made clear that music is an enjoyable activity, and that occasionally it can be solely for fun. However there are deeper reasons for music than just superficial relaxation. There is an important difference between recreation and education; school music instruction belongs in the latter category.

Most educators need to think carefully about the kind of message they give the public in terms of publicity. The public often thinks school music is comprised of marching band shows and musicals. Music educators should not undo their efforts to educate people about the music program by what they present to the public in performances and publicity.

The need for some degree of balance in what people see of the music program has several implications. For one, it means that all aspects of the program are included, at least to some extent, in what is presented to the public. In addition to polished performances by the advanced performing groups, general music classes should show what they are doing, and theory classes should present some of their original works. In other words, performances should help educate the public about the value, scope, and overall purpose of the program.

People also need to be educated about the significance of competitions among per - forming groups. In too many cases, school administrators and communities have gained the impression that winning high ratings at a festival indicates a top quality music program. They should be informed that such ratings represent an evaluation of only one small segment of the music education program. The larger portion of the program can be evaluated only on its own merits, not by inference from another aspect of the program.

If the entire music program is to be evaluated (and it is hoped that it will be every so often) then people need some guidance in doing this. The Music Educators National Conference has published *The School Music Program: Description and Standards* for this purpose. It contains suggestions of the types of things that students should know and be able to do at various grade levels, and it offers recommendations for scheduling, equipment, and other matters that are needed to make it likely that those goals can be achieved. This comprehensive view of music education not only helps both music educators and lay people to examine and compare their music programs, it also educates them about the nature of a quality music program.

There are compelling reasons for including music in the curriculum of all school students. Music is valuable for its contribution to the quality of life, and no young person should be deprived of an adequate education in it. Music educators must state the reasons for music in the schools in a way that people can understand and actually make an effort to educate them about how those reasons are being met.

Points to remember

1. The value of the music instruction for school students needs to be explained to nonmusicians in terms that are understandable.

2. Music study may result in some gains in areas other than music. However, a solid case for music instruction can be made without claiming any nonmusical values.

3. Both objective data and subjective feelings can be employed to promote positive feelings toward music among nonmusicians.

4. The main theme to be sounded when seeking support for school music should be based on a simple premise: "Let's not cheat the kids."

5. Music needs to be taught in a systematic and organized way by trained teachers.

6. The public assumes that the school music program consists of what it sees in public appearances. A careful and persistent effort is needed to inform non - musicians about both the desirability and the nature of a quality school music program.

District Administrators
and School
Board Members

Members of the board of education, the superintendent, area supervisors, and other district administrators can all have great impact on the music education program. Although recent trends show that state governments have exercised increasing authority over the curriculum, local school boards continue to control schedules, elective options, allocation of resources, and other critical aspects of the school program. For this reason, music educators must develop effective strategies and techniques for influencing local school boards and other school officials who carry out the policies adopted by them. Music educators in a school system should work within the system by observing established policies and procedures. In all cases where there is a responsive administration and board of education, they can reasonably expect to play a significant role in establishing goals and objectives for their programs. They can also expect their plans, recommendations, and concerns to receive appropriate attention and consideration.

The board of education is involved in decision making in varying ways. Generally their involvement depends on the size and complexity of the system. In some smaller situations board members may actually participate in the hiring and firing of personnel, negotiating salaries, and other managerial functions. In these kinds of operations teachers might find themselves communicating and dealing directly with board members about programs and operations as well as upper-level administrators. In most larger systems communication and direct contact with the board tends to be more limited, and because of time and other restraints, such contact takes place within carefully observed procedural guidelines. The function of various administrators also differs from system to system. Easy access to and frequent interaction with upper-level administrators can facilitate music educators' efforts to influence priorities in the school program. More restrictive and infrequent contact tends to work the opposite way and typically requires more careful planning and more formal presentations.

How should a music educator or a group of music educators go about promoting music education? The answer to this question depends on the administrative structure for music education. If there is a supervisor, director, or coordinator for the overall music education program, then this individual is certainly expected to take the leadership role and individual teachers should work under that direction. In systems that have no person officially designated for this position, music educators should request that the superintendent identify a person from among them to assume that role.

If neither a director nor coordinator of music education is available for immediate consultations, then decisions, critical evaluations, and judgments may be made without complete and accurate information or without the authentic advocacy that can be provided only by a competent professional in the subject area. The consequences are usually detrimental to the program. Even in systems that have only one or two music teachers, it is essential that someone function in this capacity.

Another key to success is determining where the decision-making power lies. Officially it is with the board of education. However, because of their backgrounds or personal interests, certain members of the board often are more influential than others, and this is where music educators should direct their efforts. If, on the other hand, the board tends to rely most heavily on whatever the school administration recommends, trying to work directly with the board is unwise. In some situations, decision making is affected significantly by the community. An individual or a group may influence decisions made by the board and the school administration. Determining where this power lies may be extremely difficult or even impossible, and it certainly requires a careful and sensitive approach on the part of the music educator. It is obvious that the cause of music education can be advanced only if those mounting the effort take into account how the system works.

Although no situation is ideal, music teachers must always commit themselves to the ethical behavior required of professionals. When efforts to communicate through established channels fail and there seems to be no other recourse, teachers may determine that the risk involved in going directly to other power sources is justified. Before making such a serious decision, music teachers should be sure that they have allowed the school system administration ample time and a reasonable opportunity to deal with the problem. They should also be sure that their information is correct, that their facts and figures are accurate, and that they have the rest of the department behind them. Depending on the nature of the problem, they may need to enlist the help of parents, arts council members, teacher organizations, and others.

Preparation

Whether music educators are speaking as administrative leaders or as individuals, they must be well prepared. Being prepared means being at least as well informed about the topic in question as the school officials and board members. All pertinent facts and figures should be clearly in mind. Depending on the matter under consideration, it may be important to be informed about enrollment trends, details of financial support, curriculum changes, accreditation, and college entrance requirements. It is also helpful to know what support other school systems are providing for music (especially those in the same region). Music educators should determine as accurately as possible what support there is within the local community for music in the schools.

The media have widely reported what prominent national studies (for example, *A Nation at Risk* and the College Board's *Academic Preparation for College*) have said about the status of public education. Some states are altering their educational systems to reflect the recommendations in the reports. However, their recommendations for student involvement in a strong fine arts program at the high school level have been largely ignored. For example, the College Board states, "Preparation in the arts will be valuable to college entrants whatever their intended field of study," and lists the arts, (including music) with science, mathematics, English, and foreign languages as the five basic areas of preparation (*Academic Preparation for College*, 1983). Music educators should make every effort to see that the entire story is presented and that state and local education agencies consider all the information contained in those reports as they implement educational reforms.

Music educators must also be knowledgeable about what national educational leaders are recommending for the elementary and high school curriculum. Respected authorities in education have made strong statements supporting the arts in the public high schools. For example, in *A Place Called School*, John Goodlad lists the arts as one of the five basic areas, and he recommends at least 15 percent of the instructional time be devoted to the arts (Goodlad, 1983). Some prominent college presidents have recommended the arts as essential preparation for college work. Music educators should draw upon these resources when talking with school officials and board members about music curriculum, music instruction, and participation in music activities.

References to "my programs," "my performing group," or "my students" are detri - mental if they create the impression that the students participate in the music program for the teacher's benefit. Rather, students and their welfare must be the special interest of educators, and school officials and board members should never be given any reason to doubt it.

Communicating with the superintendent

In most school districts the superintendent is in a position to make or break a music program. The superintendent's attitude toward music instruction in the schools affects budget allocations, curriculum decisions, time allocation and scheduling, and working conditions. The superintendent tries to make decisions that are acceptable to the com - munity, the board of education, teachers, other school employees, and students. In the last few years superintendents have felt great pressure to improve the quality of the public education system, and increasing numbers are making decisions that may deemphasize elective programs. In this day of technological emphasis, electives in the fine arts are especially vulnerable. While many superintendents provide admirable support for music programs, there are some who feel compelled to provide more math, English, social studies, foreign language, science, and computer study--at the expense of the arts. In this kind of setting it is essential that superintendents be able to say with confidence that the music program is providing something of value for students. They should be able to talk about the quality and worth of the program in specific terms and affirm that music courses are providing students with valuable learning.

Music educators can help their superintendents adopt a supportive position by communicating with them regularly and explaining the use of time and resources for music education. The following ideas may be helpful:

1. The best means of communication are reports, written at least once a year (preferably more often), especially in larger systems where regular personal contact is difficult. These reports should include brief statements reinforcing basic philosophy, goals that have been established for the program, and plans for attaining those goals. Strengths and weaknesses of the music program should be described, and proposed plans for improving the program should be outlined. It may also be appropriate to mention program needs, a current assessment of progress toward goals, and a projection of where the program will be five years in the future. Music educators should provide reports of this kind whether or not they are officially requested. All reports should be clearly written and grammatically correct. It is advisable to have someone review the report before final typing.

2. Short executive summaries in addition to the formal reports are especially effec - tive. This format provides the opportunity for music educators to emphasize the most important points they wish to make. It also lets the superintendent know that they are aware of the limited time in a busy administrators' schedule. See appendixes I and II for samples of executive summaries.

3. Invitations should be extended for the superintendent to attend an in-service meeting with music educators. Other opportunities, such as an informal lunch or dinner, provide an excellent setting to cultivate positive relationships.

4. Opportunities for contact with the superintendent may arise spontaneously. Be prepared to take advantage of the chance to promote your cause, but be considerate, diplomatic, and, above all, sensitive to the setting and circumstances. Do not, for example, complain about the limited funds available for equipment while you are engaged in conversation at a purely social event.

5. Complimentary comments about the music program from parents, students, and others in the community should be shared with the superintendent. This kind of communication can help a superintendent remain aware that the music program is valuable and that it is meeting student needs.

6. Invitations should be extended on a regular basis to the superintendent to attend special musical presentations, particularly those that are principally educational in character. Some superintendents may be more inclined to attend if asked to make brief comments or to be involved in the program in some manner. Send reserved seat tickets and pertinent information well in advance of the event, and write a letter of appreciation afterward.

7. In some cases, other individuals may represent the superintendent in making certain determinations. Curriculum administrators or directors of elementary or secondary education could be contacted by music educators for assistance.

Communicating with board members

In most school systems, direct and official communication with the board of educa-tion is maintained through the superintendent. Music educators can enhance this process by providing well-prepared reports and information that may be easily incorporated in presentations or materials given to the board. Periodically a major presentation that represents the entire arts program should be given to the board in a public meeting and should offer an opportunity not only for verbal and written reports but also for slide or video presentations or brief performances by students. If these opportunities are not provided in the existing operating procedures of the board, music educators in the system should request the opportunity to make such presentations.

Another effective approach for informing board members is to have information read into the board minutes (if the rules and procedures of the board permit). Asking the board to make special awards to music students and teachers and to pass resolutions related to music also helps to focus attention on the music program.

Communicating with curriculum directors and supervisors

When communicating with curriculum directors and supervisors it is essential to speak in terms meaningful to them. It is important to show how music is similar to English, math, and other disciplines, but also how music is different. It will be helpful for curriculum directors and supervisors to understand that music is an academic discipline with unique characteristics. Music educators should stress the value of music study regardless of a student's future plans or intended field of study. Curriculum directors and supervisors need to be reminded that music is a basic area of study that also can engage the imagination and foster flexible thinking. Along with these qualities, music can provide distinctive ways of understanding human nature.

Other administrators also need to understand the value of music education because they also can provide important help. Among this group are communications, personnel, business, and staff development administrators.

The need for positive relationships

It is critical that music educators establish and maintain positive, constructive relationships with district administrators and boards of education. It may be necessary to initiate systematic communication and procedures that will ensure a continuing flow of information about the music program. This is particularly true if there is no director or coordinator of music education in the system. Music educators should assume that administrators and school board members want to know about the music program, and they should provide information that includes goals, objectives, and recommendations for problem solving and general improvement. As a general rule, the more information that is furnished about the program, the greater the chance of support from those individuals and groups will be.

Points to remember

1. Music educators must develop effective strategies and techniques for influencing local school officials.

2. When establishing communication patterns, it is important to determine whether the power lies with the board or with the superintendent.

3. Music educators must be well informed on pertinent topics when addressing administrators or community leaders.

4. Music educators can help superintendents adopt a supportive position for music education by communicating with them through written reports on a frequent and regular basis.

5. Music educators can communicate with school board members either through the superintendent or directly, whichever is determined more appropriate.

6. Music educators should communicate with curriculum directors and supervisors on a regular basis.

School Principals

It is important that the music educator keep the school principal and assistant principals current about the music education program. The effectiveness of the music program on all levels will relate directly to the support of the principal.

Functions of the principal

The functions of the principal are to provide leadership, facilitate change, enhance school quality, and manage all professional and instructional activities within the school efficiently and effectively. The extent to which principals carry out these functions depends on how well informed they are.

Leadership

William Rutherford studied leadership skills of elementary and secondary school principals in Texas and found that the most effective principals "have clear, informed visions of what they want their schools to become--visions that focus on students and their needs." (*Phi Delta Kappan*, September 1985)

Written goals and objectives

Information about music education takes the form of clearly stated goals and objectives that focus directly on the students and their musical needs. It is best that these goals and objectives be presented to the principal in written form along with a discussion that centers on how they can be accomplished through cooperative efforts of the principal, music educators, and school community.

Change that enhances the quality of the music education program

From year to year the ideas, methods, and perhaps even the goals and objectives of the music educator are subject to change. These changes in thinking have an impact on curriculum, scheduling, materials, and sometimes personnel. Effective principals want to be abreast of changes and should be kept up-to-date in writing. When alterations in basic concepts lead to requests for major changes in curriculum and scheduling, these requests should be made at least one year in advance of implementation. Clear justification in writing along with a personal conference will facilitate the principal's ability to effect changes that can improve the music education program. It should be remembered that the effective principal expects and welcomes new ideas from all teachers. Music educators must not be reluctant to inform the principal of new ideas, but must keep in mind that time and preparation are necessary for changes.

Management of activities

Music activities are a normal part of any music education program from the primary grades through senior high school. These activities include rehearsal and performances of music groups, trips away from school, excused absence from classes during the school day, changes in class schedules, and many other functions that can be potentially disruptive. Disruption of the school day can be avoided only by careful management. All alterations caused by music activities must be worked out with the school principal. Clear communication and ample lead time are mandatory to ensure optimum use of time, facilities, and resources. Music educators can assist principals in meeting this responsibility by planning in advance for special rehearsals, group trips, movement of pianos, and other potentially disruptive events. Given time, principals can inform other teachers and staff who will be affected.

Functions of the assistant principal

A recommended standard for the appointment of assistant principals is that such positions would be warranted when the school enrollment exceeds 400. The respon - sibilities of assistant principals generally are determined by their principals. Functions assigned to assistant principals include:

1. Taking responsibility for operation of the school in the absence of the principal.
2. Serving as a representative of the school in lieu of the principal.
3. Participating in parent conferences in matters of school discipline.
4. Performing special assignments.

Music educators must exercise judgment when dealing with such matters as pro - gram changes and management of activities. Whether or not assistant principals may handle such matters depends largely upon the specific duties and authority assigned to them. If there is only one assistant principal, that individual is usually viewed as being second-in-command and can make important decisions pertaining to curriculum and activities. When there are two or more assistant principals, their titles may reflect specific responsibilities (for example, assistant principal in charge of attendance or in charge of student activities). In such cases, music educators must deal with the proper administrator.

It is difficult to overestimate the importance of proper communication with princi - pals and assistant principals. The need to keep principals informed is basic to any success on the part of music educators. Principals can be the strongest source of sup - port available to music educators.

Points to remember

1. The functions of principals are to provide leadership, facilitate change, and manage activities within the school.

2. Goals and objectives should be submitted in written form to the principal.

3. Changes in the music education program should be expected. Clear justification in writing will help inform principals of the reason for proposed changes.

4. Principals are primary managers for all school activities, although duties relating to these activities may be delegated.

5. Determine what authority and assignments the assistant principals may have with respect to the music education program.

School Counselors

Two scenarios

Jim Brown, band director at Mason High School, is visibly upset. He has just learned that his first chair trumpet player and seven other key members will be unable to participate in band next semester because their advanced chemistry class will be scheduled during the same period. Jim has experienced problems like this before, but not on this scale. When Mr. Williams (the former school counselor) was at the school, he and Jim had never agreed on matters related to the music program. Jim had hoped that the new counselor would be more understanding of the band's needs. "He's just as stupid as Mr. Williams was," Jim says to himself, "He's taking students out of the music program, now that I have the talent to produce the best band I've ever had. Even if all he understands is a bunch of psychological lingo, I'm going over to his office and give him a piece of my mind." Bursting into the office, Jim belligerently exclaims, "What are you trying to do, ruin the band?"

Ensuing events do not alter the situation. Although annoyed at Jim's rudeness, the counselor points out that all schedule conflicts should have been resolved a week earlier--as a memo to the faculty had stated. "Now you want us to revise the whole schedule just for you," he says coldly. "I'm not going to recommend it." As Jim storms out of the office, the counselor thinks, "That band director is a real dunderhead. He never reads his mail. He wants only the best students, and he thinks the entire school program revolves around him. If he were half as good as he thinks he is, he could teach some of our poorer students something about music instead of demanding only the best. It's not my fault that students want to take classes that conflict with band. It is not my fault, either, that he never bothers to check on the schedule until it's too late."

Obviously, the poor relationship between the band director and the school counselor clouds their thinking about what is best for the students.

Fifteen miles away, Bob Smith, band director at Taylor High School, is relieved. He has just been able to resolve a scheduling conflict that would have seriously weakened the band the next semester. Bob had always made it a practice to become acquainted with the school counselor, and when Mr. Williams moved from Mason High School to Taylor High School, he immediately established a positive working relationship with him. Because of this, he had become aware of a potential scheduling problem and had worked closely with Mr. Williams and the assistant principal to resolve the problem. As Bob leaves the office, Mr. Williams thinks, "What a pleasure it is to work with him. He's not like Jim Brown at Mason High. Bob anticipates problems and works cooperatively to resolve them." At Taylor High School the band director and school counselor work together to achieve a common goal of providing what is best for students.

While the preceding vignettes deal with only one area of concern, scheduling, they do underscore the desirability of music educators working closely with school counselors to achieve the best possible program of study for each student. Unfortunately, some music educators fail to recognize the importance of this relationship. They need to understand the counselor's role and how they can help the counselor become more effective in dealing with students in the music program. The following information is presented with that purpose in mind.

Duties of the school counselor

School counselors are usually classified as part of the support staff whose function is to facilitate instruction. A counselor's typical duties include:
1. Academic counseling on a regularly scheduled basis.
2. Personal counseling on a demand basis.
3. Working with teachers to resolve scheduling or achievement-level placement problems.
4. Working with parents of students experiencing academic or behavior problems.

School counselors should have as their major concerns the developmental needs, interests, and problems of the students with whom they work. They should view each student as a unique person responsible for making decisions and accepting the consequences of those decisions. They work to identify students with special abilities and needs and seek to channel their interests into classes and programs appropriate for them. Providing information about school offerings, educational opportunities, and career development occupies a considerable portion of their time. Counselors understand that the complexities of the contemporary school program make some conflicts unavoidable, but that an important part of their role is to resolve conflicts when possible. To that end, they promote positive relationships with other faculty members to aid in the optimum development of students.

Duties of the music educator

Music educators are classified as part of the instructional staff whose major function is teaching. A music educator's typical duties include:
1. Providing instruction in instrumental, choral, or general music.
2. Helping students explore and develop their capacities in music.
3. Providing a cultural setting for the school and community that promotes positive responses to music.

4. Working with parents of students participating in music to improve students' music experiences.

Music educators have as their major concerns the musical needs, interests, and problems of the students with whom they work. They should view each student as a unique person whose musical competencies they help to develop to the fullest. They identify students with unusual musical talent and seek to channel these students into classes and programs appropriate for their talents. They provide information about music offerings, musical opportunities, and careers in music to their students and the school. Music educators must understand that the music program is one facet of the complex contemporary school program and that conflicts may be unavoidable, but that an important part of their job is to resolve conflicts when possible. To that end, they promote positive relationships with other faculty members to help in the optimum development of students participating in music.

Common concerns

Because of the nature of their jobs, music teachers and school counselors often approach problems in different ways. This factor plus various conditions in the school may be causes for conflict. When this happens, it is important for each to understand the philosophy, purposes, goals, and position of the other. The manner in which the two groups work may differ, and these differences must be considered. In attempting to resolve conflicts, it is essential that the overriding consideration of those involved should be a concern for the student. Both music educators and counselors should try to develop avenues of communication. They are both part of the school and both should be interested in its activities and its successes. Schools are successful when all concerned are interested in what is best for the student.

Scheduling

It is very important that music teachers keep in close touch with counselors regarding scheduling practices. This point was emphasized in the preceding vignettes, but it bears repeating because of its importance to the music program. Care should be taken that single sections of required classes are not scheduled at the same time as performing ensembles, and an analysis of the impact of the next year's tentative schedule on the music program should be undertaken early enough so that adjustments can be made before the schedule is firmly set. It is hoped that the problem of students having to choose between music and another desired subject does not arise, but this problem is less likely to develop if music teachers and counselors work together in scheduling music activities.

Student interests

Despite the most careful cooperative planning, situations may arise in which students are required to make choices between participation in music and another class. When students are faced with such a choice, the student should determine what he or she wants to do. Questions such as "Which will do me the most good?" "Which do I want more?" or "Do I need those extra credits enough to drop orchestra?" should be used to arrive at a decision. One factor that has influenced students' decisions is a misunderstanding as to the use of the music credits for admission to college. Parents, students, and school counselors need to know that colleges and universities do accept credits in music for admission.

Level placement

When there are several levels of music classes or performing groups, students can be placed in the appropriate class or organization only by the music teacher. A policy to this effect needs to be established and applied strictly. The practice of assigning students with inadequate skills and backgrounds to performing organizations without consulting the music teacher should not be allowed. Since this affects the music teacher's efficiency, it is his or her responsibility to take the initiative in the development of such a policy with the school counselor and other appropriate school officials.

Degree of involvement

Some students may become so involved in music that they have little time or energy for other subjects. Allowing this to happen can be a disservice to students, particularly the musically talented who will need sufficient credits to attend college. Seeing that undue involvement in music does not occur is the joint responsibility of the music teacher and the school counselor.

Value of music credits

The amount of credit awarded for music study in high schools varies throughout the country. Likewise, use of grades for music in computing grade averages varies widely. As a consequence, students in music classes may not be rewarded for their achievement in the same manner as students in other academic subjects. Because this situation exists in many school systems, school counselors and music teachers have a responsibility to keep themselves informed about state and local regulations and to do everything possible to ensure that music is treated as an academic discipline and that grades for music study are weighed the same as grades for other subjects.

Relationships within the school

In some schools, competition between faculty members, departments, and courses exists to an alarming degree. Caught in the midst of these rivalries, students are often placed in difficult positions. The professional ethics of those who engage in these practices are questionable. The music teacher, while desiring to maintain sufficient enrollment in classes, should not engage in unethical practices. Instead, the music teacher should work cooperatively with the school counselor to ensure that the interests of the music program are safeguarded, and both should encourage the principal to take action that will minimize rivalries.

Class misbehavior

Many problems of misbehavior result from poor student attitude and are handled by the principal or the assistant principal. Since music classes are generally electives, the initial attitude toward them usually is positive, and misbehavior is likely to be either a personal problem affecting the student in all classes, or a communication problem with the music teacher. In either situation, counseling is more likely to be helpful than punishment. In the first situation, the counselor can serve as a coordinator of information from the home, other teachers, and the music teacher, using information from these sources to solve the problem. In the second instance (where there may be a specific clash with the music teacher), the counselor can serve as a impartial third party to help resolve the conflict.

Careers in music

Music teachers and school counselors should cooperate in providing students with appropriate information about careers in music. The music teacher should be knowledgeable in this area and should advise the school counselor about materials available for this purpose. Students should be made aware of the wide variety of music careers. Publications from MENC and the American Music Conference dealing with careers in music should be obtained and made available to high school counselors and placed in all high school libraries.

Assisting students in choosing a college or university for further music study is another area in which cooperative work can take place. School counselors may have college and university catalogs available, and they can speak in general about university requirements, but they probably will require the help of music teachers in explaining some of the specifics of music study. Counselors should consult the music teacher before directing students away from college music study.

Working together

Music educators and school counselors should work cooperatively to achieve what is best for students. What effect should this have on the approach used by music teachers as they work with counselors to achieve this end? In general, they should keep in mind that they are talking with, not at, professional colleagues who possess specific skills and information that can be used to solve problems.

Often, when time is at a premium or emotions are high, a calm and reasonable approach to problems may be difficult to achieve. One way to set the right tone in dealing with counselors is to ask him or her, "Do you have time to help with a problem?" This question demonstrates a respect for counselors' schedules, which, like those of music teachers, are busy ones. Music teachers know how they feel when someone interrupts a rehearsal and demands attention immediately. A counselor also may be facing a crowded schedule. Given the opportunity to say, "I'm really busy. Can I see you in an hour or tomorrow during your planning period?" the counselor will probably give the music teacher more time, attention, and help than if the music teacher had insisted on a conference immediately.

Often the counselor can say, "Certainly, come on in." The music teacher can then say, "I need your help with a problem." While some may consider this a weak approach, it is actually the opposite. In the first place, it is honest. The teacher does need advice, and there is a problem. Second, the teacher is complimenting the counselor by suggesting that he or she is able to help. Finally, the teacher is demonstrating wisdom and self-confidence by admitting need for help in solving the problem. Remember, the insecure person cannot admit insecurity or weakness.

Having set the tone for a successful meeting, the music teacher can then spell out the problem as clearly as possible. Quite often a solution becomes apparent simply in the telling. In any event, the presentation should be as complete as it needs to be, without repetition or self-justification. Once the presentation is over, listen carefully to the reply. After the counselor has responded, say, "What I hear you saying is... " and sum up what was just said. Then respond by saying, "According to what you say,... is right." In this way, if there are any misunderstandings, they are detected immediately. At the close of the conference, a good summary procedure is to say, "All right, in the next two days I'm going to... and you will...," restating the specific actions that will be said, taken, or written by both parties. The verbal summary helps clarify and assign specific responsibilities for the future. A written summary of the conference by both participants should be placed in the school files.

Points to remember

1. Read and respond to your professional correspondence promptly.

2. Seek the development of a positive relationship with school counselors.

3. Keep aware of proposed schedule changes.

4. Try to anticipate problems.

5. Try to understand the school counselor's point of view when problems arise.

6. Work for the development and implementation of a policy that assures placement of students in music organizations and classes by the music teacher.

7. Help students understand the desirability of a balanced educational program.

8. Do not allow yourself to become involved in rivalries with other teachers.

9. Work with school counselors in helping students with appropriate career goals.

10. Approach school counselors as professional colleagues.

11. Talk with--not at--school counselors.

12. Be considerate when asking for a meeting time.

13. Make use of both a verbal and a written summary after a meeting to restate the problem that has been solved.

14. Work cooperatively to provide what's best for students.

Other Teachers

Other teachers generally have high expectations for the music educator. To meet these expectations, the music educator must be a warm, friendly, enthusiastic, and creative person. The music educator must also exhibit specific knowledge of subject matter, talent, and broad interests. It is by sharing that knowledge and talent, and by exhibiting genuine interest in others, that the music educator may convince other teachers of the value of music education. By working cooperatively with other teachers, the music educator will find opportunities to demonstrate the purposes of the school music program.

Establishing effective relationships

Through the development of positive relationships, the music educator may effect changes in attitude and help fill gaps in the musical training, background, and experience of colleagues. This is the case regardless of whether the music educator's assignment is in elementary or secondary schools as an instrumental, choral, or general music instructor, as a resident teacher, or as a traveling teacher serving two or more schools.

Music educators can frequently establish effective peer relationships by engaging in the mutual exchange of professional expertise. The special talents and help of fellow teachers may be used to build the program in the music classroom as well as in performance. Music teachers may find it helpful to barter or share talents. For example, say to a colleague, "If you design and construct the set for our next production, I will sing for your daughter's wedding or chaperon your students' trip to Washington." Recognition should always be given to staff members who help. Whenever appropriate and possible, present those who help with a gift or honorarium.

At the elementary school level, music specialists should always recognize the expertise of the classroom teacher. The third grade teacher, for example, knows the developmental level of that particular age and can often help the music teacher provide for the needs and interests of a particular child or group. When talking with classroom teachers, the music educator should refer to "your children" or "our children." It is helpful to recognize other teachers' skills in music, art, drama, or movement. This may be done by asking them to reinforce and integrate music learning in the classroom by creating murals to illustrate program music, by writing poems to be used for composing songs, or by using rhythms and creative movement. Among the things all music instructors can do to develop positive relationships with colleagues include the following:

1. Write notes of appreciation.
2. Share with others those accolades that have been given to a fellow staff member.
3. Recognize faculty members' success outside the school or in nonprofessional activities.
4. Clip out newspaper articles about teachers or students and present them to the individuals as additional recognition.
5. Organize a get-together, picnic, potluck breakfast, or luncheon for faculty members in appreciation for sharing their students and for their help in developing an effective and meaningful music program.

Organization and cooperation

The job of colleagues is made easier by considerate and efficient organization on the part of the music educator. Both secondary and elementary music instructors should consult other teachers before taking any actions that will involve or affect them. For example, seek the approval of other teachers for schedule changes to accommodate special rehearsals, performances, or other activities. Other teachers also should be consulted regarding the practices and policies governing the shared use of classrooms, gymnasiums, multipurpose rooms, or other performance areas. Giving the best care to each teaching station will please teachers, principals, and the school custodian as well.

Music educators have many opportunities to help their colleagues. Although care must be taken to avoid exploiting students, the services of talented student groups (for example, ukulele players, guitar players, or handbell ringers) may be offered for community sings and other activities. Resources, equipment, and materials should be shared with other staff members. Being overly protective of school equipment may be interpreted as selfishness.

The release of students from other classes for music lessons or special activities is always a sensitive issue. However, with careful preparation the music teacher may avoid problems. When groups of students are involved in trips, special rehearsals, or performances, the music teacher should submit to the main office at least one week before the event the date, time, activity, and list of all students involved. When it is necessary to request the release of one or two students but impossible to make prior arrangements, the music teacher should send a clear, brief note to the other teacher(s) affected. Customized note paper, easily recognized as a message from the music teacher, is useful for this purpose. Students should never be asked to deliver such requests verbally.

Every music teacher should establish a few simple rules for students who are released from other classes for music lessons or special rehearsals. The following rules are essential:

1. When leaving another class to come to the music room, leave quietly without disturbing others.
2. Come directly to the music room without delay.
3. Classwork missed for a music activity must be made up and turned in on time.

These rules should be posted in a prominent place in the music room and should be shared with parents and other teachers. The music teacher should impress upon students that being released from other classes is a privilege that may be lost if the rules are not followed. This procedure, though important for all music teachers, is especially critical for instrumental teachers working in elementary schools.

Some elementary music specialists do not have their own classrooms and must travel from room to room. In this situation, the music teacher needs to establish the practice of being on time, and entering the room quietly and unobtrusively. A routine should be established for distributing books and other equipment. At the end of the music class, the music teacher should make sure that the students are ready to resume work with the classroom teacher. When possible and appropriate, the music teacher should provide the classroom teacher with transparencies or other materials needed for reinforcement or enrichment activities.

Informing faculty members

It is important for the music teacher to develop strategies for informing faculty members of music lessons and activities currently taking place in all of the music classes. This can be done in any of the following ways:

1. Compile a newsletter containing coming events or ideas contributed by classroom teachers.
2. Organize a "Teacher's Day in the Music Classroom" with invitations to attend a regular music class then change the traditional role of the guests from observers to participants by inviting them to play tambourines, claves, drums, and other classroom instruments.
3. Plan units of study with other specialists or classroom teachers.
4. Develop presentations that demonstrate the sequential development of musical concepts and skills for PTA programs and public concerts.
5. Invite teachers to special rehearsals.

6. Organize musical activities for teachers after school hours--class piano, ukulele, guitar, recorder, or handbell groups that can serve as both staff development and relief from stress.

Promotional activities can lead to good public relations as well as excellent learning experiences for students. Here are some ideas for these dual-purpose activities:

1. Honor each faculty member with an original song or parody written by students.
2. Organize and celebrate a music day for grandparents linking the past to the present.
3. Design and construct special music bulletin boards for classrooms or display areas as class projects.

Points to remember

1. Other teachers often have high expectations for music educators.

2. The music educator should establish effective relationships with other teachers through the exchange of professional expertise and the recognition of staff members.

3. The music educator should be considerate of other teachers and school programs.

4. Every music teacher should establish rules for students released from other classes for music rehearsals.

5. Elementary music specialists who travel from room to room should be on time for each class, enter quietly, and have established routines for distributing materials.

6. The music educator should develop strategies for informing other teachers of the learning taking place in music classes.

The Media

The media" is a term that elicits a variety of responses from the American public. Perhaps it is the visibility of both broadcast and print media that strikes feelings of awe, fear, or even anger at the seemingly unapproachable people called journalists. The music educator who has an important message to convey must learn to work with the media and learn the techniques for effective communication.

Know the score

There are a few basic techniques for relaying the message that music education is a necessity. Some are merely mechanical; others involve a degree of creativity and good judgment.

It is essential that music educators know what information is newsworthy. This is sometimes difficult to determine because it is a subjective decision. What one person calls news may not be so to another. The basic idea is that news must be seen from the perspective of the audience. The wider the appeal, the better the coverage one can expect.

The hook

If you are planning an event or writing a story, it is important not to forget the "hook." If the news of your up-and-coming concert sounds somewhat bland, see what you can do to reword the information to capture attention.

For example, a standard lead might be: The Riverdale High School Band will present a concert on February 18, in the high school auditorium. The 8 p.m. concert will feature the music of Beethoven.

A better lead might be: Mr. Joseph Henderson, superintendent of schools, will be featured as guest conductor on February 18 when the Riverdale High School Concert Band presents its winter concert at 8 p.m. in the school auditorium. The concert will pay tribute to Ludwig van Beethoven.

Other hooks may be employed to capture attention and broaden audience appeal. Perhaps the mayor was once a member of the school band. Asking him to present a special award might stir all kinds of interest.

Whatever you do, keep an eye out for that which is unique, either about the event, the composer, the conductor, a current or former member of the group, or the way the music is being presented. Try to relate the music to the local scene. Give it a personal touch. A home grown flavor might be just the thing you need to attract a crowd.

Preparation

Submit your announcement to the media well in advance. Waiting until the day of your big musical event to inform the media is too late. You cannot expect preferential treatment if you call at the last moment. Newspaper personnel are concerned with column space; radio and television broadcasters are locked into time restrictions. The media work with deadlines. Composing public service announcements (PSA's) or news stories to fit the allotted space is no simple matter.

If you are writing the news copy yourself, make sure your report is timely. Also, when contacting journalists by phone or in person, be cognizant of their time schedule. Pushing to make a point or failing to be considerate of the deadlines facing journalists may hinder your efforts for a long time to come.

Be objective

When writing your news story, especially when reporting something that has already happened, make it fact rather than opinion. For example, if you report that the music was beautiful, you are presenting an opinion. However, if you write that the audience gave the performers a standing ovation, you are reporting a fact, but you are also implying that the music must have been performed beautifully.

Be accurate and thorough, whether submitting copy for a coming event or writing about one that is recently past. The journalist is taught the importance of the five "W's and H" that mean who, what, when, where, why, and how. The who and what are the most important. If titles or names are included, make sure all are correct and legible. Keep a copy, lest a typographical error in an important article should return to haunt you.

Inverted pyramid

The journalist writes in an inverted pyramid style, which begins with the item of greatest importance and continues with items of descending importance. If the paper must print a story in limited space, the editor will not be as likely to cut out the heart of the story, but merely snip off its tail. Bear this in mind when preparing copy.

Layout

When you submit copy, it should be double-spaced on a sixty-space line. Type in "--more--," centered at the bottom of each page, if the story continues. At the conclusion of the story, type "--last--," "-30-," or "***" in the center of the page after the last line.

Photographs

When possible, include photographs with news releases. Action pictures are preferred. For example, a band marching is preferable to a seated group. Children in elementary school music classes make excellent subjects for photographs. These photos should be black-and-white glossy prints. If there is a choice, action pictures of one or two students are preferable to large-group pictures, because individuals cannot be easily recognized in the group photographs. An ideal spread would show one group picture and several pictures of one or two students in the act of making music.

Television appearances

With access to cable, it is more possible than ever for performing groups to appear in either full programs or in promotions for coming concerts. The music educator should be aware of the problems associated with sound reproduction for telecasts. If a good sound recording is not possible, record the video and audio separately and make use of lip synchronization during the actual telecast. However done, it is extremely important that the recorded sound be of the best possible quality.

Relevant subject matter

It is difficult to get articles in newspapers or time on the air to cover or report the day-to-day activities of a music education class. Music educators need to think of clever ways to get instructional activities presented in the media in place of the typical coverage of band trips, parades, festival rankings, and the like. For instance, the profession is well-served by coverage of activities such as children singing songs of many nations in celebration of United Nations Day. In certain parts of the country, a story about student exposure to "country fiddlin'" as a means of learning certain important violin performance techniques is of great interest. There are many other important aspects of music instruction that are interesting and newsworthy.

Headlines

Be aware that headlines are written by someone other than the article writer. When this occurs, there may be some degree of misrepresentation or distortion of the essential message. It may help to suggest a brief headline of five or six words utilizing an action verb highlighting key elements of the story.

The news interview

The music educator should be very careful about what is said to reporters and other media representatives. As a rule, the conversation should be of a positive nature. Above all, avoid attacking superiors, colleagues, or the school board. Get clearance from the proper authorities before discussing or releasing sensitive information to the media.

Negative interviews do not help the music education program, and indeed, may lead to generally poor media relations. A worthwhile music program can be damaged by careless remarks, to the detriment of students, music support groups, and arts lovers as a whole.

Disappointment is possible

Even after a great deal of preparation by music groups, parents, and others, and in spite of the great anticipation of reading or viewing stories about the music program, these stories may never appear in the media. Editors do cut material, and music education stories may be removed from the paper or television news script to make way for late-breaking stories. For this reason, students, parents, and anyone else inter-viewed by media personnel should be warned of the possibility that their story may never appear. Such a forewarning may prevent great feelings of disappointment if the music story is cancelled.

It is vitally important for music educators to develop good media relations. The media and the music educator can help each other. They both exist to serve the public.

For more information on how to communicate effectively with the media, refer to the 1984 MENC publication, *Promoting School Music: A Practical Guide.*

Points to remember

1. Try to view your situation from the media's perspective.

2. Learn what is newsworthy or reword your approach to make your effort newsworthy.

3. Understand the mechanics of writing in good journalistic style.

4. Be factual and accurate.

5. Be timely.

6. Be professional and considerate.

Parents

The parents of students enrolled in a school music program are usually the best source of community support for the program. In most instances there is no need to convince these parents of the value of the music program. Given an interest in music and a desire to see their children participate, it remains that they be well informed about the music program and that their energies be channeled in the right direction.

Informed parents as advocates

In order to become good advocates, parents should be knowledgeable about the goals and objectives of the music program in which their children are enrolled. It is the responsibility of the music educator to help parents develop this knowledge. Information can be disseminated in general newsletters, meetings planned for parents, special-interest group meetings, classroom demonstrations, attendance at rehearsals, and by other means. As part of any orientation for parents, there should be general discussion and a demonstration of a particular aspect of music education.

Music educators must spell out the objectives at each level for general, instrumental, and choral music. It is essential that these objectives reflect a balanced view of the music curriculum and that this view be understood by the parents. When talking to a specific group of parents (for example, parents whose children are in an elementary general music class) the music educator might discuss the work taking place in the general music class and show how it contributes to the realization of later goals. To improve communications, the goals and objectives of the music program should be available in printed form and given to all parents as they enter the meeting.

Discussions with parents should always be two-way affairs. Parents should be considered when the music curriculum is being developed. There is much to be said for having parents on the curriculum committee when developing a music program. There have been cases reported in which the desires of the parents were not reflected in the efforts of the music educators. Barbara Kaplan reported in the *Alabama Project Project Seminar*, "Music Society and Education in America," that 48.6 percent of parents surveyed considered music reading a desirable area of study for their children. The music educators involved were surveyed, and only 12 percent of them acknowledged efforts to develop music-reading skills. (University of Alabama, 1984) This is a case in which communicating with parents could have led to better information for the music educators and, ultimately, a music education program more to the liking and benefit of all concerned parties. Two-way communication is essential if informed and enthusiastic support for the music program is to be generated.

When parents are enthusiastic about the the music program and believe strongly in it, they should be encouraged to speak in support of music not only at PTA and school board meetings, but also at meetings of teacher organizations and chambers of commerce. In addition to communicating with groups outside the school, it is important that parents inform the principal that this interest runs much deeper than their support of the more spectacular events such as band and choral public appearances.

Class visits

In addition to structured orientation sessions, parents can learn about music education programs directly through class visits. During such visits the parent should be permitted to take part in music making or class discussions as much as possible. For example, a parent could spend some time seated in the clarinet section next to his or her child. A mother or father could sing along in the alto or bass section with the student in a choral rehearsal. Parent involvement in Suzuki programs is already a well-established practice, and similar parental involvement should be encouraged in general music classes. During or following a class visit, opportunities should be arranged to permit parents to ask questions about any aspect of the lesson of the day or about the music program in general.

Evaluating and grading

Parents frequently ask about grading in music classes. Both parents and students want to know the basis for assigning grades. They are also interested in related matters such as sectional seating and participation in festivals, contests, and other competitions. Music educators should utilize grading criteria beyond attendance and promptness in getting to class. The criteria should be in written form. In addition, music educators should make clear the effect of absenteeism and discipline problems on the grade. Parents should be informed as to how much homework and practice is expected of their children.

Attendance at performances

If attendance of students is mandatory at public performances and if grades will be affected by missing these performances, the parent must be informed in writing when the student enrolls in the performing group.

Adjudication sheets

Adjudication sheets for district and state festivals and other group evaluation summaries should be displayed and explained to interested persons. How ratings are awarded, factors considered on adjudication sheets, festival ratings, and so on, can be clarified during parent meetings. The evaluation process used to select students for all-state, honors programs, and the like should also be explained.

Private lessons

Many music educators encourage students to study music privately. Both music educator and parent should be aware of school district policy regarding this practice. If private study is a factor in awarding grades to students, this should be clearly explained. It is important that state laws and school district policies pertaining to music educators teaching their students privately and for pay be clarified and made public.

Parent organizations

The most influential support groups for music education programs are the various parent groups. These may include groups such as the local PTA and booster groups specifically organized to support performing organizations in the school. The PTA can give support, guidance, and the benefit of established leadership that smaller groups may not possess. Parent-supported groups will also receive more support and cooperation from all involved if they work cooperatively with the PTA in their efforts.

Experience has shown that a booster group is most effective when the following guidelines are observed:

1. The music educator exercises appropriate leadership in the group.
2. The purpose of the group is clearly stated and understood.
3. Fundraising is not the only purpose of the organization.
4. An effective means of communication is maintained between music educator, students, and parents.

The music educator as leader

Booster groups can be valuable for the music program if they have proper leadership. Most of the difficulties with booster groups have developed when the music educator has been reluctant to take the leadership role, thus allowing well-meaning but often misdirected persons to lead the group. These problems can be avoided if the music educator properly informs the parents involved that booster groups are part of the overall music program and are, therefore, under the direction of the music educator. In MENC's national Music Boosters program, the music director serves as a valuable liaison between the school and the chapter president.

Clarity of purpose

With the leadership of parent groups clearly established, it becomes easier to explain the purpose of the group to its members. Once the purpose is clearly under -

stood, there is less likelihood of individual members expending time and energy in inappropriate endeavors. Members of parent organizations can serve as "time savers" to the music educator, volunteering as chaperons and uniform distributors, participating in letter and telephone campaigns, or writing newsletters.

Fundraising

Almost every parent group faces the task of generating additional funds to assist in pursuing the goals of the music program. Indeed, fundraising is the sole reason for some organizations' existence. This should not be, and the music educators should communicate this fact to the group at organizational booster group meetings. Moreover, it should be stressed that instructional programs included in the school curriculum should be supported by school funds. The more relevant reasons for the existence of the booster group should be emphasized by the music educator. One way of accomplishing this is to incorporate in each meeting of the organization some music education-related subject other than, or in addition to, fundraising. Such subjects might include goals and objectives of the music education program, evaluation, private lessons, and the purchase and maintenance of musical instruments.

Fees

If music fees are required, parents should be informed that the school system has approved this practice. Music fees are not permitted in some school systems, and music educators should adhere to local policy. Music educators should explain to parent groups how the fees are used and what policy is applied for students who are unable to pay the fee. Some parent booster clubs provide funds for students unable to pay music fees.

The importance of communication

Communicating with parents is an important part of the music educator's job. It is not easy to find adequate time for this task, but it is a job that must be done. Parents who enroll their children in music classes want and expect good music experiences for their children, and most are willing to do their part to bring about these experiences. It is the task of the music educators to guide them in this effort.

Points to remember

1. Parents should be informed about the goals, objectives and content of a quality music program.

2. Informed parents make better advocates.

3. Communicating with parents is an essential part of the music educator's job responsibility.

4. Parent groups should work cooperatively with the PTA for a unified effort rather than competing with them.

5. Booster groups can be a valuable aid to the music educator if handled correctly.

6. Music educators should adhere to the school district policies regarding fees.

The Community

The community is a large and important constituency that music educators should inform about the music education program. Members of the community vote in school board and tax levy elections, contribute funds for music projects, and attend performances. While they may not be as closely involved with the music program as are parents or school administrators, the sheer number of people in the community makes it an area that music educators should not ignore.

How can music educators inform the community? The techniques and procedures will vary according to the size and characteristics of the area. Regardless of the size of the community, its artistic and educational aspirations and traditions are of great importance. Here are some general suggestions that can be applied to most communities.

More than bumper stickers

Music educators must communicate to the community what the music program is about and what students are learning through it. This means going deeper than a superficial, "bumper sticker" level of awareness. A shallow consciousness of school music is probably better than nothing, but it is not enough to motivate people to support a quality music program. Slogans like "Support School Music" have an effect only if the individual is already inclined to favor music in the schools, and a slogan alone does not say anything about what school music is or how it should be supported.

Performances

The main contact that most people have with the school music program is through performances. In addition to presenting programs in schools, school music groups perform for service clubs, march at football games and parades, and appear in other events. Performances offer a tremendous opportunity to develop interest in and support for the school music program. A successful performance probably accomplishes more in terms of engendering support than a thousand words about the virtues of music study.

Performances are, however, a two-edged sword. They can be very helpful, but they can also be detrimental if not carefully prepared. Several principles should guide music teachers in planning and carrying out performances. These principles are as follows:

1. Performances should be an outgrowth of the study of music that takes place in the class or rehearsal room. School music groups do not exist to give performances; they perform because they have learned and wish to demonstrate that learning. The educational purpose of school music should always be given priority.

2. Performances should be properly prepared so that the music is performed as well as possible, given the age and musical experience of the students.

3. Performances should present music of quality that is appropriate for the occasion. Just as one does not feature Beethoven's *Fifth Symphony* at a basketball game, one should not sing the latest country and western music at a performance of the advanced choir.

4. Performances by a group should be limited in number and scope so as not to interfere with other components of the curriculum.

5. Performances should include all members of the class or group, and not feature only the more talented students. Again, school music groups exist for the education of all students.

6. Performances should be well managed in terms of getting the performers on and off the stage, the deportment of the students, the placement of the piano, and all the other details that can affect the impression a performance gives.

7. Performances should be interesting and informative, and should instruct the audience about both the music performed and the music education program. Imaginative teachers have come up with a number of ways to present music: a variety of music can be performed; a few simple actions can be added; informative comments can be offered by students or the teacher; some simple props can be used; and the order of the program can be arranged to elicit the maximum response at its conclusion.

Other practical ideas for music teachers to consider in making performances more effective include:

1. Asking all or some of the audience to participate in one or two numbers by singing or playing along.

2. Asking alumni of the performing group to join in for one traditional selection.

3. Asking accomplished musicians in the community to conduct one number, or to otherwise participate in a performance.

4. Sending out complimentary tickets to school administrators, board members, and other persons who you hope will attend the performance.

5.   Publicly recognizing all who assisted in producing the program, especially custodians, stage hands, and cooperative teachers.

There are many chances to perform in most communities. In fact, there are so many that it may be necessary to establish some procedures for keeping the number of performances within reason to preserve the integrity of the educational program. This can best be accomplished by working well in advance of actual requests for perfor - mances and by establishing policies regarding places to perform and limits to the number of performances. (Refer to the 1986 publication, *Guidelines for Performance of School Music Groups: Expectations and Limitations*, available from MENC.) A community organization whose reasonable request cannot be honored during the current year can be scheduled for the next year. Requests that cannot be fulfilled must be turned down tactfully and with an explanation.

Fundraising efforts

A way in which many members of the community have contact with school music programs is through the students who sell candy, concert tickets, or other such items. It is difficult to evaluate the effects of this kind of contact with the general public. On the positive side, it does make the community more aware of a portion of the school music program, and in many communities these efforts have raised sizable amounts of money. There are some negative things to consider, however:
1.   The contact does little to inform people about the music program.
2.   Only one portion of the program is involved. In fact, such efforts often rivet the attention of the community for months on only one organization, to the detriment of the rest of the music program.
3.   The music program is put in the position of publicly admitting that the activity is not supported by school funds--something that is not true of most curricular activities. Fund drives are usually related to extracurricular activities-- cheerleading, athletic uniforms, trips, and the like.

No two people react in the same way to solicitations by school students. However, it is difficult to see how fundraising drives have a beneficial effect on a community's commitment to a quality music education program. This is one of the reasons that extensive fundraising efforts should be avoided.

Music In Our Schools Month

A successful public relations activity of Music Educators National Conference over the past decade has been Music in Our Schools Month (MIOSM) each March. The idea is to give school music greater visibility by focusing attention on it for a specific period of time. Publicity is generated not only by individual school systems, but also by state and national organizations through proclamations from governors and mayors, television and radio spots, and posters, pins, and other awareness items.

The potential of MIOSM for promoting greater community consciousness about school music is substantial. The music teachers in a particular district can coordinate a series of programs under the MIOSM banner, and some districts use the occasion to form all-district performing groups. The specified time period also gives newspapers and other media an angle for stories and spots. An especially newsworthy activity is the **World's Largest Concert**, a live television broadcast involving nearly one-half million students. Some businesses permit the use of space on advertising signs. Other businesses allow posters, either developed by MENC or created by students, to be placed in windows or on walls. Any district whose music teachers are not taking advantage of MIOSM is missing out on a ready-made opportunity to improve the status of its program in the community.

Being active in the community

One of the most effective means of developing support for school music is for music teachers to be active members of the community. Personal contacts can open doors for informing people about music education and securing opportunities for school groups to perform. Busy music teachers should find time to join community organizations, including some that are not in arts or music. At times such participation will include holding an office or other leadership position.

Developing support from specific groups

A community is made up of many groups, each with its special interests and concerns. Several of these groups are particularly important and logical ones for building community support for music education, because their members already value music and the arts. Therefore, they need only to be recruited as active supporters of the local school music program.

Professional musicians

The interests of most professional performing musicians in regard to the schools lie in preventing school groups from usurping jobs that are rightfully theirs, and securing some employment with school students in terms of performances or private lessons. The first concern about the proper roles for professional musicians and student musicians is longstanding. In 1947, it led to the development of the Code of Ethics by the American Federation of Musicians (AFM), the American Association of School Administrators, and MENC. The code has been renewed periodically since that time, and is available from MENC. It is also discussed in the MENC publication *Guidelines for Performances: Expectations and Limitations* and some music education textbooks.

The provisions of the code are quite logical. Performances for commercial or partisan events (playing for the opening of a new Sears store or at a campaign rally) are the province of professional musicians, while educational and civic events are the province of school groups. Music educators should follow the provisions of the code not only because it is the ethical thing to do, but also because it can contribute to good relations with a segment of the community.

The second interest of professional musicians, that of securing work performing in the schools or teaching, also can significantly affect relationships with them. Logically, professional musicians and music educators have a similar goal in terms of a vital musical culture. Some professional musicians are adept and interested in performing for school students. When feasible, the school music program should include programs by Young Audiences, "Artists in the Schools," and similar projects. These joint efforts can enrich the school program, provide work for the performers, and give the performers a positive feeling about the school music program. To involve professional musicians, music educators need to be in contact with them. A few minutes discussing mutual interests at a meeting of the AFM local can be time well-spent. If there is no union in the community, musicians should be contacted individually.

A professional or semiprofessional orchestra exists in many communities. Again, both the school and orchestra can benefit from working together to provide educational experiences for the students. Such cooperation engenders support and respect for the music program from an interested segment of the community.

Virtually every community has church choirs. Opportunities for joint performances with one or more good choirs should not be overlooked. They can involve and encourage the support of another group of interested community members.

Private music teachers

Music educators and private music teachers should work closely for the benefit of the students they serve. Music educators should encourage their students to study privately for increased challenges. Private teachers can help the school music program by coaching accompanists, soloists, and small ensembles. Through such organizations as the National Guild of Piano Teachers and the Music Teachers National Association, private teachers may act as support groups for school music programs.

Many school districts allow credit toward graduation for private music study undertaken by high school students. In these districts, there are carefully developed rules and criteria for the approval of private teachers and the evaluation of student progress. All school districts should maintain a list of approved private teachers. With carefully developed standards and procedures for compilation of these lists, only competent teachers will be included and recommended. Music educators should always recommend all of the competent private teachers in the community.

College music educators

Another source of interested and informed support in some communities is the music education faculty at a nearby college or university. It is surprising how little use is made of this resource by many school districts, even when it is readily available.

When they work together, college and school music educators can accomplish a great deal. The college teachers can often supply useful information, and they have a national perspective that is very difficult for school music teachers to achieve. In addition, they are probably more experienced in preparing written materials. On the other hand, schoolteachers can provide concrete examples of the nature and value of music in the schools, and they understand their particular situation much better than college faculty members.

The most important thing to achieve in getting school and college teachers working together is a sense of equality. Neither group should create the impression that it is superior to the other. Prejudices should be laid aside. College teachers in music education are not usually out of touch with the "real world" of school music, and school music teachers are seldom lacking in intellectual or musical abilities.

Music merchants

No one has a more direct interest in the success of the school music program than the person who sells instruments and music to school students. Music merchants are a logical source of support for music education. Music stores are not all the same, of course. Some sell band and orchestral instruments, while others concentrate on electric guitars and related materials. However, the more active the market for school music materials and equipment, the more likely the stores are to carry these materials and to be interested in the school program.

Music educators should be careful to deal with all music merchants in an ethical manner. Schools should purchase music equipment and materials on the basis of clearly specified bids, all music stores that deal fairly with their customers should be recommended, and music teachers should not accept gratuities or commissions from music merchants. In other words, the relationships with the merchants should be on an open, professional basis.

Arts organizations

Another group in the community that should be especially supportive of the music program are those persons involved with arts councils and similar organizations. Methods for working with this segment of the community are presented in chapter nine.

Service clubs

In many communities, organizations such as the Rotary, Kiwanis, and Lions Clubs provide a valuable avenue for informing the public about the school music program. Furthermore, their members are often leaders in the community. Ask permission for a school ensemble to perform at a meeting. On such occasions it would be possible for the teacher to include some information about the music program, such as the fact that the group earned a superior rating at contest or festival, that it is learning about Handel and oratorios, or that two of its members are going to enter college next fall as music majors. Service clubs can also be a source of financial support for special projects in the school music program.

A coalition for school music

It may be possible to bring together representatives of various community groups to form a comprehensive association or coalition for school music. As the old saying goes, in unity there is strength. By working together, parent groups, music merchants, private music teachers, and other groups can be more effective than each operating on its own. Although school music teachers may provide the impetus for the coalition, they need not accept the formally designated positions of leadership. They certainly should avoid the appearance of forming an organization to ensure the longevity of their own jobs. Rather, the purpose of the coalition is to see that students have a balanced, quality program of music education--the "Let's not cheat the kids" approach mentioned in the chapter one.

The exact composition of a coalition will vary considerably from one community to another. In any case, it should be as broadly representative as possible. If the organization is large, it should have an executive board that can act expeditiously. In addition, it needs to have a clearly thought out program of action. People do not like being members of groups that limp along with no clear purpose.

The actions of a coalition will depend on the local situation. It may be that an information campaign needs to be mounted to establish a climate of support for school music, or that action is needed to support particular segments of the program that appear to be vulnerable to cuts in time or financial support. Another function of a coalition should be applying information about what is needed for a quality music program. Local music teachers should work with and advise the members of the coalition on such matters.

A coalition should be a continuing group. It should work to advance music education even when no urgent problem exists. In this way, the prospects for crisis situations are greatly reduced.

1. Informing the community means giving people something more than an awareness of the school music program.

2. If handled properly, performances can build community support for the music program.

3. Fundraising drives should be limited, because they tend not to build continuing or informed support for the music program.

4. Full use should be made of MIOSM and the media.

5. The personal contacts that music teachers develop as active members of the community are an effective means of informing people about the school music program.

6. Many groups in the community have members who already believe in the value of the arts and music. They are much more likely to support music education. These groups include professional musicians, private music teachers, college music educators, music merchants, and people active in the various arts organizations.

7. In many communities it may be possible to bring these and other interested persons together in a coalition to speak for music education with a unified and strong voice. They can help promote music in the schools.

Arts Organizations

The music program in any school benefits from close cooperation with arts organizations. Millions of people in America support and promote the arts through local, state, regional, and national arts organizations. Music educators should become involved in these organizations, thereby increasing awareness of local school music programs and their needs.

National organizations

The network of support for the arts in America includes a number of national organizations. Important among these are the National Endowment for the Arts, the Alliance for Arts Education, the United States Department of Education, the National Federation of Music Clubs, the National Foundation for Advancement in the Arts, MENC, and other professional organizations. (See appendix III for addresses of these organizations.)

The National Federation of Music Clubs has programs of special interest to music educators, such as National Music Week. The National Foundation for Advancement in the Arts sponsors a talent search and awards grants of $500 to $3,000 to high school seniors who are seventeen to eighteen years of age and who have demonstrated excellence in dance, music, theater, visual arts, or writing. Others have programs and activities of value for music educators.

State organizations

Each state and territory has an agency or governmental department responsible for the arts and cultural affairs. This agency or department can assist with national and regional programming and can initiate its own state programs. Artists In Education is a program that is fairly common to all state arts agencies. It provides an opportunity to bring performing artists to the schools for residencies of varying lengths of time. The state agency may permit residencies for composers or arrangers to work with music groups or with theory and composition students. Interdisciplinary, international cultural exchange programs and state touring programs are also available and are a valuable source of enrichment for the music curriculum. These programs are offered through grants to local arts agencies or schools.

Arts educators are also served by the state Alliance for Arts Education, an advocacy association that monitors legislative activity, supports legislation, and seeks increased appropriations for the arts. This group can be an important voice in the state legislature and thereby a vital link in the political process of improving arts education.

Local organizations

The National Endowment for the Arts and most states now define a local arts agency as an organization that serves all art forms in a local community through service to cultural groups in individual arts and qualifies as a not-for-profit corporation, or a government arts agency officially recognized by a county or city government. State agencies can identify local arts agencies and the services they offer.

Community-based interdisciplinary umbrella organizations that serve the arts exist in every state. These organizations may be branches of local municipal government (for example, city, county, or city/county cooperative councils), private not-for-profit community organizations, organizations founded through special legislation, or private organizations serving the arts. Arts organizations may also be organized as agencies of state governments, such as arts commissions or cultural affairs offices. Some are independent public agencies. In some instances the arts are served at the local level by the municipal recreation department or the public library.

There are similarities among local arts agencies, but there are also differences. Some have memberships, and some do not. Some of the boards of directors are appointed, while others are elected. Some receive monies from special taxing districts and special taxing sources. Others are partially or fully funded by public monies, while some depend totally on private funding. All seek additional funds to support, develop, and nurture the arts.

The local arts agency is a valuable resource in the community providing a variety of services. Among these are:
1. grants
2. workshops on funding, services, and programs
3. a clearinghouse for dates or an arts calendar
4. cultural resources center and library
5. artists and organizations directory
6. newsletters, promotion, and publicity
7. artists' job programs, registry, referral service
8. volunteer professional services
9. tutors
10. block booking, central box office for local theaters
11. consulting
12. meeting, rehearsal, and performing space
13. multidisciplinary arts festivals

14. career information and services
15. speakers bureau
16. competitions, awards, scholarships, scholarship information
17. advocacy
18. arts classes for adults and children
19. computerized mailing services
20. slide presentations
21. publications
22. programs inside and outside the school
23. special services and projects

Working with arts organizations

When people beyond the school community are interested and involved in music education, good things can happen. Funding may be provided for special projects, partnerships with businesses may be developed, or laws and policies may be written to provide for development of model educational programs.

Working with local arts organizations is important for music educators, but such a venture is always a two-way street. Both must have a sincere desire to work together toward common goals. Each must recognize the value of providing genuine service to the other, and each must respect the particular interests, expertise, and responsibilities of the other.

Preparation

Before approaching the local arts organization for assistance, music educators need to be prepared. This preparation should include:

1. Studying *The School Music Program: Description and Standards* (available from MENC), and comparing its recommendations with the local school music program. Any discrepancies should be listed as "needs of the school music program," and these should be arranged in order of priority. Those needs for which the local arts organization might provide assistance should be identified.
2. Developing a list of services that the school might provide for the local arts agency. For example, music educators can announce local concerts and activities of the arts organization. Music educators might also encourage student participation in workshops or as volunteers.
3. Discussing with the school principal the needs of the music program and the possibility of involving the local arts organization in meeting them. With approval of the principal, the music educator will be ready to approach the local arts organization.

The first meeting

The initial contact with the executive director of the local arts organization should be a personal visit, set by prior appointment. Call before the meeting to confirm time and place. During the meeting, write down important information about programs and services that can be of benefit to you.

Learn what services and programs are available locally and elsewhere. The local agency will have complete information on programs available to help the music educator. Discuss the particular needs of the school program with the executive director of the local arts agency.

Follow up with a letter describing any action agreed upon at the meeting. Ongoing communication to all concerned is important, and copies of all correspondence should be sent to those who need to be kept informed.

Collaborative projects

When planning cooperative ventures with a local arts agency or organization, look at the goals and objectives of the music education curriculum. In what areas is assistance needed to reach the goals? Use the arts organization to supplement school resources, not supplant them.

If a need exists for scholarships for talented students, enlist the aid of the local agency to locate business and corporate support. The agency might organize a competition to determine the scholarship recipients. It could also assist with fundraising through contacts in the community, business, or in trust departments of local financial institutions. This sort of cooperative project provides wide visibility as well as the needed financial assistance.

Concerts or assembly programs for the school may be a priority. Compare the impact of single appearances by local or nationally known artists with a long-range residency of a composer or arranger. Look for programs and projects that will have a major impact on the school program. Recitals and concerts need to be scheduled appropriately in the scope and sequence of educational activities. Such programs are available through local arts agencies. These organizations may be able to locate a musician from a major performing group or a college music professor who would like to work with students over a period of time. If a touring artist is brought to the schools, students should be prepared for the event through lectures or demonstrations. The local arts agency can arrange in-depth preparation before, and follow-up after, a residency or performance.

Artists and local organization personnel visiting the school should always be introduced to the school principal and given an opportunity to chat informally with him or her. These visitors may reinforce ideas previously voiced by the music educator.

The local arts organization may be interested in arranging a television program featuring a panel discussion of arts education in schools. The organization might also be able to sponsor a conference at which standards and model programs are discussed by teachers, school administrators, parents, and local citizens. Such activities bring the resources of the school and the organization together and they generate interest in the improvement of educational programs.

Many arts organizations sponsor festivals, workshops, and special events for the community. Music educators and their students may benefit from participation in these programs. They may also assist with mailings, distribute posters and announcements, or serve as ushers.

Local arts organizations often publish newsletters, directories, and calendars of local events. Music educators should contribute to these publications and ask to be placed on the mailing lists to receive them.

While curriculum development is typically the responsibility of the school or district, any local curriculum committee for music education could well include one or two lay members that represent the community. These citizens could be nominated by the local arts organization. The organization might provide meeting space for such a committee. They might also be able to help with printing curriculum documents or workshop materials.

Most local arts agencies are partially funded by federal and state grants. Because of this, they have an official credit statement including the National Endowment for the Arts, the state arts agency, and local support. This is a legally binding agreement between them and their granters. Make sure that this credit is used on all publicity and promotion for any cooperative venture. However, the official credit statement usually can be amended to include school supporters as well. Be sure to recognize the support of local, state, and national legislators whose appropriations made a program possible.

Points to remember

1. Millions of people in the United States support the arts through local, state, regional, and national arts organizations. These groups form a network that can provide support for school programs.

2. National, regional, and state arts organizations have programs of interest to music educators.

3. Local arts agencies and organizations provide valuable resources for school and communities. They may help to locate funds and programs to meet local needs.

4. Working with the local arts organizations can provide reciprocal benefits for music educators.

5. Prepare for the first meeting with personnel of the arts organization by identifying the needs of the music program, preparing a list of services the school can offer, and discussing program needs and possible collaborative projects with the school principal.

6. Use the first meeting with the personnel of the arts organization to learn about their projects and to discuss the needs of the school music program.

7. Collaborative projects can include providing scholarships; arranging programs; providing residencies; preparing television programs or conferences; participating in locally sponsored arts events; using newsletters; directories and calendars to publicize arts events; and involving representatives of arts organizations in school committee work.

8. In any collaborative venture, be sure to use the official credit statement of the local arts agency and to recognize all funding sources.

Government Officials

Many government officials are interested in music and quality education. Many of them remember positive musical experiences from their own school days and may still participate in music activities. Others acknowledge that they had little musical training in school but are eager to see that today's children have a music education.

Government officials are usually pleased to have the opportunity to appear at school events in their hometowns. During such events they learn about the status of education and the needs and achievements of those they serve. It is appropriate for any music educator, with the approval of the school principal, to invite the local mayor, council member, legislator, congressman, or other official to take part in a special school music event by narrating a portion of a special concert, making a presentation at an awards banquet, or conducting a special selection at a concert. This sort of involvement by government officials provides good publicity while also keeping the officials informed of the value and scope of the local school music program.

Music educators have a responsibility to inform government officials about values and purposes of music education so that a balanced program can be provided for all young people. When local school administrators, teachers, parents, and citizens are convinced of the worth of an educational program, they are more likely to carry the message to their elected officials.

Local officials

A basic understanding of the roles and the responsibilities of the mayor, county council, and local board of education is important to the music teacher. Because the determinations of local school boards and local governments are of such vital concern to music educators, chapter three covers to this subject.

State officials

Whenever a state law, policy, standard, rule, or regulation appears to be violated or misinterpreted at the local level, it is essential that facts be verified and accurately reported. In such instances it is important for the music educator to work through the state music educators association to correct the problem. Each state association has a government relations committee responsible for studying problems and issues at the state level, framing position papers for adoption by the executive board of the association, planning appropriate courses of action, and coordinating the activities of individuals in order to bring about needed changes. It is in the best interests of music education for the state association to present an image of strength and unity to all government officials. These officials have different roles and responsibilities. Understanding what these are helps music educators to make appropriate appeals for assistance when needed.

State music supervisor

The state music supervisor is an employee of the state and a member of the state superintendent's staff. As a public servant, the state music supervisor acts as a liaison to the state music educators association and may serve as an ex-officio member of the association's executive board.

The duties of the state music supervisor are varied. These duties may include:

1. Designing, developing, implementing, monitoring, and evaluating the state music curriculum.
2. Providing in-service training for teachers.
3. Planning conferences and meetings.
4. Developing student achievement tests and other evaluative instruments.
5. Working with accreditation teams for local school districts and institutions of higher education.
6. Writing reports and preparing budgets.
7. Drafting policies, rules, and regulations as directed by the state board of education.
8. Preparing documents or information for committees appointed by the state board of education (for example, state textbook adoption criteria).
9. Providing technical assistance and information to local school districts, institutions of higher education, professional organizations, and individuals.

There are things the state music supervisor is not permitted to do. For example, the state supervisor does not hire music teachers, purchase supplies and equipment for schools, make policy decisions, act as a lobbyist, interpret state laws, or have authority to dictate a particular schedule of music classes for a local school. On the other hand, it is part of the state supervisor's job to provide accurate information or advice on any matter concerning music education.

To obtain information from the state supervisor, a music educator needs only to pick up a telephone. The state supervisor's name, address, and telephone number appear in the state education directory available in every local school and district office. Many matters that may seem complex and unusual to a music teacher often can be handled easily by telephone. However, there are occasions when a personal appointment is necessary. To make an appointment for a meeting with the state supervisor, a call to the office may be made, but one should not be disappointed if it cannot be arranged immediately. When asking for an appointment, state what is to be discussed so that both parties can be prepared for the meeting.

If a question arises concerning a state law, policy, standard, rule, or regulation, the state music supervisor should be contacted before any action is taken. Accusations should not be made. Facts should be stated, then advice requested. All written material sent to a state office should be accurate, keeping in mind that correspondence with government officials and government files are public records.

Every music educator should work cooperatively with local and district school personnel, calling upon the state supervisor for information, advice, and expert assistance when needed.

State superintendent of schools

The state superintendent of schools holds an office that in thirty-three states is established by the state constitution. The duties of the chief state school officer are defined by the constitution or by statute. Broadly stated, these duties are to supervise and direct the public schools of the state. The chief state school officer is empowered by the constitution or by statute to interpret both laws and policies pertaining to public education in the state.

An individual music educator may encounter a situation in which a superintendent's interpretation of a state law is needed for improvement of a local music program. For example, the music educator might find that the elementary music textbooks used in the schools are more than twenty years old and in very poor condition. The music educator might ask the local administrator or state music supervisor about state laws and policies governing the adoption and purchase of textbooks.

Should the music educator discover that state law requires local districts to adopt current textbooks in a prescribed manner, but that the language used in the law is vague regarding required purchase of those textbooks, a legitimate request for a super-intendent's formal interpretation may be made. However, the individual music educator should exercise caution, because making such a request could antagonize local district administrators. It may be advisable for the music educator to refer such a situation to the president or government relations chair of the state music educators association. The officers of the state association may know of other teachers experiencing the same problem. After compiling all known facts of the matter, the association president may write a formal request to the state superintendent for interpretation of a specific law or policy.

The state supervisor of music should be informed of any request sent to the state superintendent. This will increase the likelihood that all the facts are made available and that a fair, objective interpretation is written. The state superintendent's interpretations are then made public and distributed to local district superintendents.

Requests for information, mailing lists, and documents should not be sent to a state superintendent; neither should letters expressing personal opinions. All requests and letters are referred to members of the superintendent's staff, and those regarding music education are referred to the state music supervisor. Time and tax dollars are saved when letters and requests are sent directly to the state music supervisor.

Officers of the state music educators association often have opportunities to involve the state superintendent in musical events. The state superintendent may be invited to speak at a state convention or all-state concert, to participate in the presentation of special awards, to pose for pictures with award winners, to prepare and distribute a memorandum concerning MIOSM, or to introduce a special MIOSM concert at the state capitol. An invitation to attend all-state concerts should always be sent to the state superintendent. When asking a state superintendent to participate in any event, the association officer responsible should notify the state music supervisor and give all the details about the activity. This allows the state supervisor to arrange for appropriate publicity, to check the superintendent's schedule, making sure that the proper place and time have been noted, and to send the proper background information to the superintendent.

Whenever a state superintendent of schools appears on a state association program or provides a memorandum announcing an association-sponsored activity, a letter of thanks should be sent by the association president.

State board of education

The manner of selecting members to state boards of education differs from state to state, with some boards elected and others appointed. Members of some boards are chosen to represent specific areas of the state. Regardless of how the membership is selected, the state boards of education are responsible for determining educational policies and implementing laws and policies relating to education. Policies adopted by state boards have the force of law.

State board policies may be initiated by board members, professional organizations, the legislature, the courts, other agencies, or individuals. Policies are drafted, critiqued, and reviewed by the staff of the state department of education. Following these steps, the state board frequently appoints an ad hoc committee of school personnel to study the proposal and make any changes deemed necessary. The proposal is then sent to the state board where it is debated and, if it is accepted, distributed for public comment or hearings. Comments received are compiled and studied by the department of education staff and the ad hoc committee. The committee may then recommend changes for consideration by the board. Once a policy has been adopted by the state board, it is distributed to local school superintendents, other education agencies, and concerned individuals.

State organizations seeking to initiate new policies should first secure support from parents, community people, other education organizations, and several state board members. Such support is necessary to assure the approval of any proposal brought to a state board of education. For example, one association brought to a state board a request for a formal policy requiring that high school credit be granted for private music lessons. The board rejected the proposal. Before that ruling was made, any local school system in the state could grant such credit; after the ruling, it became illegal to do so. It is not enough to make a proposal or a presentation to a state board of education; the organization must also demonstrate broadly based support for the measure.

State boards of education frequently permit professional organizations and civic groups to make presentations at regular meetings. The president of an association wishing to make such a presentation should write to the executive secretary of the state board (usually the state superintendent) and ask to be placed on the agenda. This request should be sent as much in advance as possible.

A presentation to a state board of education should be carefully planned, clear, concise, and accurate. A brief written report should be given to each board member. Bearing in mind that board meetings are long and tiring, presenters should not be discouraged by any seeming lack of attention by members of the board. Accomplishments as well as needs should be stressed by those addressing the government board. Music educators must take care to send the right message: Music education is important and valuable for all students.

While any music educator can comment on a proposed policy during a comment period, the state music educators association may take a formal position and ask its members to submit comments consistent with and in support of that position. When policies affecting music programs are under consideration, it is essential that the state association adopt a position and use its government relations network to send appropriate comments. The comments should address only the specific policy under consideration and should be carefully written. A coordinated and unified effort is impressive; on the other hand, a wide diversity of opinion tends to confuse policy-makers.

The state music educators association should consider involving state board members as well as the state superintendent of schools in musical events. State board members may be invited to speak at conventions, to present awards, to write short articles for the state journal or newsletter, and to participate in special MIOSM activities. Whenever such invitations are accepted by a state board member, the state music supervisor should be informed so that appropriate publicity and arrangements can be made.

Board of regents

The governing body of the state system of higher education may be the state board of education or a separate umbrella board (variously called regents, governors, and so on). Where there is a separate board of regents, its procedures and functions will be similar to the state board of education.

While primarily concerned with higher education, a board of regents may adopt regulations having dramatic effects upon public education. For example, college entrance requirements determine, to a large extent, the course offerings of public high schools. The state music educators association should monitor the proposed policies that come before this governing board and be prepared to respond to them.

As is true of other state officials, boards of regents members may become more knowledgeable about music education by participating in activities sponsored by the state association. They should be invited to take part in state events, particularly those that feature music in higher education.

The legislature

Legislatures of the fifty states differ in their exercise of authority over public education. While one state's legislature may pass a law specifying the teacher/pupil ratio for various grade levels and particular classes, another state's legislature may pass a law requiring the state board of education to set such standards.

Music educators should not rely on legislators for support when important issues are the subject of debate, if the legislators know nothing about music and its value in education. Legislators need and want to be well-informed on all topics of interest to their constituents.

Local music educators should look for opportunities to provide information regarding the purpose and value of music education to the state's lawmakers. One way to do this is to inform local representatives when school music groups perform at the state capitol. Legislators often make special efforts to attend these events and to pose for pictures with students. If asked to speak briefly to the students, legislators may make statements supporting music education that can be used later in the press. Individual legislators may provide tours of the capitol or printed material describing the state's government for students.

Efforts by music teachers to influence state legislation should be coordinated by the state music educators association. There are three reasons for this. First, the government relations chair of the association is familiar with the state education code, the structure of the legislature and its committees, and the procedures to follow. Second, MENC and its affiliated state associations are tax-exempt organizations whose lobbying activities are governed by state and federal laws. Finally, the association may adopt formal positions on legislative issues, publicize those positions widely, seek the support of other organizations, and determine an appropriate course of action to be taken. Legislative activity requires careful planning and the concerted efforts and time of a great many people.

The state association can ask members of the legislature to participate in special functions such as those suggested for the state superintendent and members of the state board of education. This kind of activity helps to keep both lawmakers and music educators informed of each other's concerns.

The governor

The state governor is responsible for preparing the state budget and presenting it to the legislature. Generally, the governor has power to veto the budget passed by the legislature. In some states, this power of veto may extend to specific line items in the state budget. This power of the governor should be of critical concern to music educators in whose states there is a separate line item for music education outside of the statutory formula for public school support. In states where this is the case, the music educators association should attempt to develop strong ties with the governor's office as part of the government relations program.

A state association officer who wishes to arrange a meeting with the governor should first send a letter of request explaining the purpose of the desired meeting. Approximately ten days later, a call should be placed to the governor's appointment secretary. It is wise to allow ample lead time when requesting an appointment with a governor. One should also be prepared for the possibility that the appointment may have to be canceled at the last minute, or that a member of the staff may substitute for the governor.

The governor or the governor's spouse also may be asked by the officers of the state association to perform ceremonial functions, such as issuing a proclamation for MIOSM, attending a special concert given in conjunction with the fiftieth anniversary of the founding of the state association, or sending congratulatory letters to students receiving national recognition. Activities of this nature are valuable in bringing music education to the attention of the governor and members of his or her staff.

1 Inviting government officials to participate in local school music events provides firsthand information to the official and the opportunity for good publicity.

2. Individual music educators should work within the state music education association whenever laws or mandates of government agencies are concerned.

3. When working with government agencies, it is essential that all facts be reported accurately and clearly.

4. The state music supervisor should be called upon for information, advice, or expert assistance.

5. The state superintendent of schools can be asked to interpret specific laws or policies affecting music education, but the request is best made through the state music educators association.

6. Whenever policies affecting music programs are being considered by the state board of education, the state music educators association should adopt a formal position and use its government relations network to send appropriate comments and information.

7. The governing body of the state system of higher education sometimes adopts regulations that affect music education in the public schools.

8. The state music education association should coordinate efforts to influence legislation affecting music education.

9. In states in which there is a separate line item for music education outside of the statutory formula for school support, the state music education association should work to develop strong support from the governor and his or her staff.

10. The governor, chief state school officers, members of the state board of education, board of regents, and legislature may be invited by the state music education association to participate in conventions, meetings, concerts, or ceremonial events.

The Challenge

Establishing a quality, comprehensive music program in a school or school district is no easy task. If it were, there would be no need for this publication, and almost every school throughout the nation would have a well-balanced music program with adequate equipment and materials and sufficient time for instruction.

Why does securing adequate support for a quality program usually require a great deal of effort and thought? Basically the problem lies in the fact that school boards and administrators, and to some extent society-at-large, have limited resources with which to support the many subjects in the school curriculum; they simply cannot do everything they would like to do. Clearly, the greater the amount of funds available, the greater the prospects for a quality music program. However, even when resources are reasonably adequate, school boards and administrators must make decisions about the extent to which they can support each subject-matter area.

The factors that affect the amount of support a subject receives are complex. They range from subjective impressions about what parents and the public desire to the personal values and interests of the people making the decisions.

Can music educators exert some influence on the decisions related to their field? Absolutely! The actions they take and the information they provide can have a real impact on the amount and type of support given a music program in a school or state. Can music educators always succeed in having decisions come out as they want them to? No. No matter how great the need or how solid the logic of their case, there are times when valid and justifiable requests are not supported. Being right does not mean that one always wins. Being right, and proceeding in an intelligent way to achieve an objective, means only that one's chances for achieving success are greatly improved.

What should music educators do when they are unsuccessful in an effort to maintain or improve the quality of music education? First, they should wait a few weeks for emotions to cool down. Then they should examine as objectively as possible the tactics and materials that were used to see how they might be improved for another try. It may be that a slightly different approach is needed or that additional constituencies should be enlisted in the effort. The chances of learning precisely why a proposal was not supported are slim. An analysis of the situation usually produces some probable areas for improvements, but it is unlikely that you will be able to pinpoint the reasons as to why you were not successful.

Second, after the postmortem on the unsuccessful effort, make plans for another try at the next opportunity. Perseverance is one of the keys to success in securing a quality music program. This is true for several reasons. The decision makers sometimes need to consider a matter more than once. They rarely have the background and understanding of music that music teachers possess, and they have many other matters to consider, so good ideas often require an incubation period before they are supported. Sometimes the circumstances that contributed to a failed effort change enough to make a subsequent proposal successful. For example, a principal or board member who was unsupportive may be gone when a proposal is resubmitted, or more funds may have become available. A second (or third or fourth) try has added impact because the administrators or board members are impressed with the steadfast commitment to the proposal on the part of the music teacher; they become convinced that it is not a spur-of-the-moment desire.

There are also some actions that music educators should not take if they are unsuccessful in achieving a positive response. For one, they should not adopt an attitude that the persons making the decision are stupid or mean-spirited. Educators should not assume that all is lost and that there never can be any improvement. Neither should they begin bad-mouthing the persons who made the decision or become chronic complainers; such actions only make the critic look bad. Finally, they should not take the lack of support for a proposal as a personal affront, at least without clear evidence. Decisions about what is best for the students should be made on the merits of the ideas, not on the personalities involved.

It is unfortunate, but in some school systems the administrators and other officials seem incapable of ever supporting a quality music program. The good news is that such persons and situations are the exception rather than the rule. In only a minority of all school districts (actually far fewer than most music educators believe) can the situation be accurately described as grim. However, to pursue the worst-case scenario for a moment, what does a music educator do if well-thought-out proposals and requests that have been presented several times have failed to receive positive action? One of two choices remain: Either accept the fact that things will not improve much (at least in the near future), and stay in that job, or seek another position that appears to offer better professional opportunities. Most people and school districts want what is best for the students in music and in other areas of the curriculum, and that means that many other more promising situations exist.

The future of music in America's schools will partly be what its music educators make of it. They will not always get what they desire in terms of equipment, time for instruction, and course offerings, but they can make a real difference in bringing about improvements in music programs. One means of doing this is to pursue some of the suggestions presented in this book for informing people about music education. Such efforts can make a difference, because people are more likely to be supportive when they are informed.

The rewards of music study for the student in the schools, and eventually for society at large, are much too great for music educators to fail to make a major effort to develop support for a quality music program in every school.

Your Role

Now that you have finished reading this book, it is hoped that you have realized that in addition to the many duties you already perform, you have an added responsibility--the responsibility of informing others about the benefits of music. The answers to all your questions may not have been found, but the suggestions given can help you deal more effectively with key individuals and groups outside music who influence the discipline. Music educators have for too long talked only to each other about their problems and concerns--it is time to talk to others.

Music educators have always been ingenuous about improving the lot of music. Music education in this country was established by persons far from the center of American cultural life and without benefit of government support. It has grown into a nationwide program that no other country can match. This growth was accomplished because our predecessors possessed strong convictions about the unique contributions of music. Now you are challenged to keep this strong tradition alive.

The future of music education in the United States will be determined largely by the actions of music educators. No other group is going to make the effort. As an individual music teacher, you should play an active role in this movement. You must do your part in following the suggestions in this book, realizing that when others are adequately informed they are more likely to be supportive of music programs.

If in your personal quest for your own humanity, you have made music a major factor in your life, you understand the need. If you value Bach and Beethoven and all the others who gave us music that raises our spirits, helps us know who we are, and teaches us to live with joys and sorrows, you understand the message. Please help convey it to others.

Appendix I

EXECUTIVE SUMMARY
Status Report on Fine Arts Program

I. **Purpose**
   A. Develop aesthetic sensitivity of all students
   B. Provide opportunities for involvement in arts performances and activities
II. **Goals - students will:**
   A. Use arts as outlet for self-expression
   B. Acquire basic understanding of artistic heritage
   C. Function in artistic roles
   E. Use arts vocabulary and symbol systems
III. **Components**
   A. General music (K-8)
   B. Choral music (6-12)
   C. Instrumental music (6-12)
      1. strings and band
      2. winds
   D. Visual arts (K-12)
   E. Theater arts (8-12)
IV. **Strengths**
   A. Excellent teaching staff (four hold doctorates)
   B. Comprehensive, objective-based curriculum guides in all areas (K-12)
   C. Supportive community and administration
   D. Increase in number of students rating high in competition festivals at system, district, and state levels
V. **Needs**
   A. Adequate teaching stations for all teachers (especially middle school strings) appropriate for their area
   B. Funding of core materials for art specialists at all schools
   C. Additional stage rigging for theater productions
   D. Art teachers at all elementary schools (two-thirds of schools have art teachers; eight are needed)
   E. Four strings teachers to fully implement program at all middle schools and high schools
VI. **Indicators**

Area	Students served	Teachers	per pupil expenditures*
Music	26,717	62	$ 2.20
Visual Arts	28,147	35	3.30
Theatre	500	9	10.20

*per pupil expenditures do not reflect teacher salaries and benefits. The cost reflects core materials and textbooks.

(Prepared for superintendent of schools by fine arts supervisor.)

Appendix II

EXECUTIVE SUMMARY
MEMORANDUM

TO: David Short, Superintendent
                  Gallaxie County Schools

FROM: Melody Sayre
                  Fine Arts Supervisor

SUBJECT: Request for increased music time allocation from Gallaxie County Music Educators
                  Association

Purpose

The Gallaxie County Music Educators Association has submitted a formal request that Policy B-20-25 be revised to provide a minimum of 7 percent of the instructional day for music in grades K-6. This memorandum provides background on that request, lists several alternatives, and recommends action.

Background

1. Guidelines in effect from 1960 through 1980 suggested that music be taught twenty minutes daily in grades K-3 and twenty-five minutes each day in grades 4-6. While these time allocations were not mandatory, eighteen of our twenty-five elementary schools were providing this amount of time in 1979. With the adoption of Policy B-20-25 in 1979, three of the elementary schools' principals announced reductions to the mandated 5 percent of the instructional day (approximately fifteen to eighteen minutes). At present, our music specialists in fifteen elementary schools see each class for 7 percent of the the instructional day; in our ten rural elementary schools, music teachers have only the minimum time with each class.

2. Increasing the minimum time allocation for general music to 7 percent of the instructional day would equalize music opportunities for all our students. As you know, students in our rural schools have consistently scored below average on music achievement tests.

3. By adopting this proposal we would meet the standards of the Music Educators National Conference that calls for allocation of 7 percent of the instructional day for a basic music program. It would also be consistent with the current education reform movement and would bring our policies and practices more closely into alignment with John Goodlad's recommendation that 15 percent of the school day be devoted to the fine arts.

4. This proposal is a reasonable one. With the decline in our student population, we would be able to implement it with our present staff plus one new position.

Alternatives

We could:
1. Reject the proposal.
2. Modify the proposal and recommend increasing the music time allocation to 6 percent (using only our present staff).
3. Recommend to the Board of Education adoption of the GCMEA proposal to increase the minimum time allocation to 7 percent.

Recommendation

I recommend the third option and ask that you forward the GCMEA proposal to the Board of Education. I will provide enrollment and teacher assignment data if you so desire.

Appendix III

Listed below are the addresses for the arts organizations listed in chapter nine.

National Federation of Music Clubs
1336 North Delaware
Indianapolis, IN 45202
317-638-4003

National Endowment for the Arts
1100 Pennsylvania Avenue, NW
Washington, D.C. 20506
202-682-2000

U.S. Department of Education
400 Maryland Avenue, SW
Washington, D.C. 20002
202-245-8707

Alliance for Arts Education
Education Department
J.F.K. Center for Performing Arts
Washington, D.C. 20566
202-254-7190

National Foundation for Advancement in the Arts
100 N. Biscayne Blvd.
Miami, FL 33132
305-371-9470

Selected Readings

College Entrance Examination Board. *Academic Preparation for College: What Students Need to Know and Be Able to Do*. New York: The College Board, 1983.

Goodlad, John I. *A Place Called School*. New York: McGraw-Hill, 1983.

Music Educators National Conference. *Guidelines for Performances of School Music Groups: Expectations and Limitations*. Reston, VA: MENC, 1986.

Music Educators National Conference. *Promoting School Music: A Practical Guide*. Reston, VA: MENC, 1984.

Music Educators National Conference. *The School Music Program: Descriptions and Standards*. Reston, VA: MENC, 1986.

Report of the National Commission on Excellence in Education. *A Nation At Risk: The Imperative for Educational Reform*. Washington, D.C.: Department of Education, 1983.

Rutherford, William. "School Principals as Effective Leaders." *Phi Delta Kappan,* September 1985.

Wolff, Karen I. "The Community as Educator: Paper presented at the *Alabama Project Seminar*, "Music Society and Education in America," University of Alabama, November 1984.